# THE BOOK OF ART

A Pictorial Encyclopedia of Painting, Drawing, and Sculpture

VOLUME 5

# FRENCH ART
# FROM 1350 TO 1850

# THE BOOK OF ART
A Pictorial Encyclopedia of Painting, Drawing, and Sculpture

# FRENCH ART
# FROM 1350 TO 1850

Edited, with an Introduction, by
Michel Laclotte
*Principal Inspector of Provincial Museums, France*

Grolier INCORPORATED

# HOW TO USE THIS BOOK

To obtain the maximum information and interest from this series it is necessary to understand its basic plan. With the exception of the first volume and the last two volumes, which are more general in their scope, each of the other seven volumes is arranged as follows:

First, a historical Introduction sets out the main lines of development within the school or period, with special reference to the major artists and the major works of art.

This is followed by a biographical section outlining the life and work of every major artist and important minor artists. The Biographies run in alphabetical order according to the name by which each artist is most generally known, whether it be surname, or Christian name (as for example LEONARDO da Vinci), or nickname (as TINTORETTO). With each biography is given a cross-reference to the page or pages on which he is represented in the plates sections which follow; a monochrome reproduction of one or more of his other works; and (where possible) a self-portrait or portrait of the artist and a specimen of his signature.

Next follow the sections of Color Plates, Drawings, and Sculpture. Each of these sections is arranged in chronological order according to the date of the artist's birth, though in a few cases minor adjustments to this order have been made for the sake of comparison or design. To illustrate painting techniques, particularly of frescoes and large easel paintings, some color plates show a detail rather than the whole work; but the use of such a detail is indicated in the caption, and a monochrome illustration of the whole work is normally given with the artist's biography; in such cases the size given in the caption refers to the whole painting. The location of every work of art is included in its caption. Every effort has been made to include also the size, medium, and date of each work represented in the plates, though this has not always been possible since not every museum has such information available for all the items in its collection. The reader will also appreciate that the precise dating of many works of art is the subject of scholarly controversy; however, no dates have been included here unless they have the authority of qualified experts and art historians.

A final section, entitled Influences and Developments, rounds off the period by drawing together the main ideas and characteristics of schools and styles, and by exploring the internal and external influences that have made their impact on the development of the arts during the period concerned.

A list of basic reference books for further reading appears on page 16. Books containing material of special interest concerning an individual artist are listed at the end of the relevant biography.

To avoid repetitive explanation of basic technical terms such as *genre, chiaroscuro, baroque*, etc., an illustrated Glossary is provided in the volume entitled *How to Look at Art*. Also in that volume is an Index listing every artist mentioned throughout the series.

Taken as a whole, the series thus provides a comprehensive, carefully integrated, and highly informative survey of the achievement and significance of Western Art from its origins to the present day.

NOTE.—The terminal dates in the titles of some of the volumes are inevitably approximate. One volume will sometimes overlap with another. Some artists mentioned under French Art, for example, are also represented under the Impressionists, and the Post-Impressionists merge imperceptibly with the Moderns. In the ever-continuous process of Art it is difficult to contain schools or periods within precise boundaries.

Designed and produced by George Rainbird Ltd., London
PRINTED IN ITALY by Nuovo Istituto Italiano d'Arti Grafiche - Bergamo
This edition printed 1985.

# Contents

## LIST OF COLOR PLATES

## ACKNOWLEDGMENTS

The publishers and producers wish to express their gratitude to all the museums, art galleries, collectors, photo-
graphers, and agencies who have courteously assisted
them in obtaining the material for the illustrations reproduced in this volume. They would especially like to thank
the following:

Albertina, Vienna
The Art Institute, Chicago
The Ashmolean Museum, Oxford, England
La Banque de France, Paris
The Barber Institute of Fine Arts, Birmingham, England
Bayerische Staatsgemäldesammlungen, Munich
Bibliothèque de l'Arsenal, Paris
Bibliothèque Nationale, Paris
Sir Anthony Blunt, London
The Trustees of the British Museum, London
The Brukenthal Museum, Sibiu, Roumania
Ets. J. E. Bulloz, Paris

Buzzachi, Rome
Caisse Nationale des Monuments Historiques, Paris
Monsieur J. Camponogara (Photos), Lyon
Château de Versailles, Versailles
The Cholmondeley Collection, London
R. Cocchi, Rome
College Governors of Alleyn's College of God's Gift, London
Comédie Française, Paris
The Courtauld Institute Galleries, London
Michel Descossy (Photos), Montpellier
The Devonshire Collection, Trustees of the Chatsworth
  Collection, Chatsworth, England
École Nationale des Beaux-Arts, Paris
R. B. Fleming & Co., London
Mr. J. R. Freeman, London
The Fogg Art Museum, Cambridge, Mass.
The Frick Collection, New York
Gemäldegalerie, Dresden
Simone Guiley-Lagache (Photograph), Paris
Kunsthalle, Hamburg

# French Art from 1350 to 1850

### The 13th and 14th centuries

After the mural paintings of the Romanesque period, and the stained-glass windows of the great Gothic cathedrals, the first notable expression of French pictorial art appeared in the small, exquisite, decorative paintings of the manuscript illuminators. A regular school of miniaturists grew up in Paris during the 13th century, and the influence of these often unknown painters, with their stylized Gothic vision of art, spread through all Europe north of the Alps.

Easel painting did not make its appearance until the middle of the 14th century. Though partly inspired by the prestige enjoyed by Italian experiments in this field, easel painting, with its larger scale, also satisfied the general European need at this time to find a more faithful mirror to nature. From this time on miniature painting and large-scale painting followed their separate ways. But the stylized Gothic forms used and developed by the miniaturists were inadequate tools for the new kind of painting produced by this artistic revolution. The French were only able to make a break with the past through the stimulus of a group of Flemish painters who had come to work in France.

### International Gothic

The naturalistic tendencies of these northern artists combined fruitfully with the Gothic tradition, and Franco-Flemish centers were established in Paris, Dijon, and Bourges. By about 1400 these had produced the most brilliant and certainly the most influential exponents of the International Gothic style—a style that also flourished in such far distant places as Prague, Valencia, Milan, Verona, and Hamburg. It was a juxtaposition of a dream-world fantasy and the drama and reality of everyday life; a mixture of extravagant graphic elegance and careful analysis of volume and space. These pleasingly contradictory trends characterized all the best practitioners of this style: the miniaturists who worked for the magnificent Duke of Berri—especially the Limbourg brothers, illuminators of the great European masterpiece, the *Très Riches Heures du Duc de Berri* (p. 85). They included also painters to the dukes of Burgundy—Jean de Beaumetz, Jean Malouel, and Henri Bellechose.

During the 1420's and 1430's, while the Master of Flémalle and Jan van Eyck in Flanders, as well as Masaccio in Italy, were opening up exciting new vistas of pictorial art, the French painters, confined to limited activities by the Hundred Years' War against England, were still reproducing the then moribund formulas of International Gothic. It was not until 1450 that the French school recovered its position; its output could never be compared with that of the Flemish or Italian schools, even allowing for the fact that many works are known to have been lost.

### The School of Avignon

The artistic revival of the second half of the 15th century first showed itself in Provence. Thanks to the influence of the Avignon Popes, Provence had already established itself as a lively center for the pictorial arts from 1340 to 1370; in the 15th century a bourgeois patronage attracted painters to Aix and Avignon from all parts of France and Flanders. Out of the ideas they exchanged, enriched by contact with Mediterranean centers, the School of Avignon was born.

Its earliest masterpiece, *The Aix Annunciation* (p. 91), painted about 1444, still shows Flemish influence. But the most impressive of the other works painted in Provence between 1440 and the end of the century—*Our*

*Lady of Sorrows*, 1452, and *The Coronation of the Virgin*, 1454, by Enguerrand Quarton (p. 86), the Avignon Pietà (p. 87), various anonymous works and, toward the end of the century, those by the Master of St. Sebastian—show marks of profound originality. The most outstanding characteristics of these works are the sharp definition of volume, the dramatic and plastic rendering of light effects, the tendency toward monumental composition, and the restrained intensity of human expression and religious feeling.

## Jean Fouquet

Jean Fouquet of Tours combined the plastic traditions of Gothic carving with the color schemes and ornamentation of the illuminators, blending with them the new doctrines of Flemish realism and Tuscan stylization (it is known that Fouquet spent some time working in Italy). Yet the soft light and peaceful countryside along the banks of the Loire suggested to him a more serene vision of the world, less poignant than that depicted by the Provençals. The manner in which he planned his historical or religious compositions, and decorated the *Hours of Étienne Chevalier* and the *Jewish Antiquities*, shows an appreciation of monumental form and luminous space that was to revolutionize miniature painting. His easel pictures reveal the same desire to give architectural dignity to painting in general. Yet there is nothing dry or austere about this architectural painter; on the contrary, he shows a lively narrative interest and a sympathetic understanding of both town and country life, as well as the lyrical powers of a great landscape artist.

## Provincial centers in the 15th century

Fouquet had several pupils who worked at Tours, like himself, or for the French court, but none of them could match him for unity or epic grandeur. Michel Colombe inherited his picturesque qualities, and Jean Bourdichon, miniaturist to Anne, Queen of Brittany, emulated his gentle charm, though he sometimes spoiled it with fussy detail. Neither of them appreciated the value of vitality and equilibrium as he did. The only artist who might be considered a rival of Fouquet's, owing to his imagination and command of style, was the Master of King René of Anjou, who illuminated the *Coeur d'Amour Épris* in about the year 1460.

While Provence and Touraine were the greatest centers of artistic originality in France during the 15th century—centers which produced art that was truly French—other regions, although more dependent on Flemish prototypes, were not inactive. The finest works painted in Paris in the second half of the 15th century, the altarpiece painted for the Parement de Paris and works by the Master of St. Gilles, were the products of artists who were trained strictly in the Netherlandish tradition. Similarly in Picardy and Artois, the altarpieces by Simon Marmion and Jean Bellegambe were in the style of Bruges or Brussels with only a thin French veneer. This was also true of some Burgundian altar-panels, though here traces of the influence of the School of Avignon can also be seen.

## The Master of Moulins

The greatest French painter of the late 15th century, the Master of Moulins, was also strongly influenced by the technique of the great Flemish masters, especially by that of Hugo van der Goes. One of his early works, the Autun *Nativity*, clearly shows this Flemish influence. Working as he did at the Bourbon court at Moulins, in French surroundings, he came under the spell of the decorative elegance and monumental clarity of the Gothic traditions of Central France—traditions which lingered in France long after the Renaissance had been launched in Italy. He far surpassed them, however, in sensitivity and imagination, and eventually followed the trends set by Jean Perréal and Jean Bourdichon, with whom some historians have tried to identify him.

## Portraiture in the 16th century

Several 15th-century painters, including Fouquet, had executed individual portraits, but portrait painting did not achieve great and lasting success until the 16th century. There are still in existence a large number of oil paintings and red, black, and white chalk drawings of French aristocrats attached to the court from the time of Francis I to Henry IV. These works can be distinguished from each other only by slight stylistic differences: they show the same over-all conception of portraiture and the same line of tradition (in spite of changes that were taking place in other branches of painting), from Jean Perréal to Jean Clouet and Corneille de Lyon, from François Clouet to the Quesnels and Dumonstiers. These artists, influenced at first by the Flemish and Lombard schools, produced an almost uniform style: their models are usually painted smaller than life size, seen almost full face, and portrayed as busts or half-length figures against a neutral background. Although the artists gave due attention to lavish costume, they concentrated on the model's face. Their subtle idealization did not prevent them from revealing the sitter's moral character, often with penetrating psychological finesse. They also showed a similar precision and delicacy of handling in their manner of outlining and highlighting solid form. In short, this is an elegant, rather conventional art whose outward monotony should not blind one to its refinements.

## The First School of Fontainebleau

While the portrait painters were active in Paris and Lyons and at the court itself, a new art was evolving in Fontainebleau. In an effort to imitate Italian Renaissance patrons, Francis I had been trying for a long time to make the French court the most brilliant artistic center in Europe—though the High Renaissance had already passed its peak and Mannerism was now the prevailing style. He persuaded Leonardo da Vinci and Andrea del Sarto to work for him, and bought paintings from Raphael and Titian. Eventually he found a leading artistic figure with ideas to match his own ambition—the painter Rosso Fiorentino, who arrived in France in about 1530 but died ten years later. Two other Italians (summoned by Henry II), Primaticcio and Niccolò dell' Abbate, continued after Rosso's death to develop Mannerist ideals in the painting of magnificent decorations in the Château of Fontainebleau and other royal residences. The Italians were joined by Flemish and French painters (such as Antoine Caron), as well as by sculptors and enamel and tapestry workers; a whole school was thus established whose influence was reflected in the work of François Clouet and Jean Cousin, and whose ramifications spread throughout Europe. This, the First School of Fontainebleau, Italian by origin, represents something more than a simple variation on Tuscan or Parmesan Mannerism. The king's own taste and that of the society around him lent color to its world of poetry, enlivened its often esoteric humanism, and accounted

for its elegant eroticism. At the same time, French and Flemish artists, following their own traditions, tempered the Italians' exuberance and softened their exaggerated plasticity, resulting sometimes in a certain dryness. This blend of civilization and style gave rise to the unusual charm of the School of Fontainebleau. Its lesson in harmonious decoration remained a basic principle of French decorative art.

## The Second School of Fontainebleau

At the end of the 16th century, the Second School of Fontainebleau was established under Henry IV, with Toussaint Dubreuil, Ambroise Dubois, and Martin Fréminet as its leading figures. Though not so brilliant as the first, it continued to express the attractive qualities of Mannerism, its unreality and its romantic fantasy. Even in the mid-17th century, draftsmen like Bellange and Callot, painters like Deruet and, to a certain extent, Claude Vignon, still belonged to the Mannerist school of thought.

## The influence of Caravaggio

Meanwhile the young French painters who were anxious to learn about newer developments went to Rome. In that cosmopolitan milieu a new mode of art was evolving under the stimulus of controversial and often conflicting experiments. The first painters to arrive, Le Valentin, Simon Vouet, and Claude Vignon, were immediately confronted with Caravaggio's revolutionary ideas: his intense, lyrical realism and his unprecedented treatment of light. Georges de La Tour's early daylight pictures with popular themes, and his later nocturnal religious compositions illuminated by a single candle, also derive ultimately from Caravaggio. La Tour managed, however, to give his silent, nocturnal groups a mysterious poetical atmosphere and a unique monumentality by the grandeur of his compositions and the skillful simplicity of his coloring.

A distant echo of Caravaggism and a more direct reflection of the minor Netherlandish masters appeared in the works of the three brothers Le Nain. Louis, who showed the most personal feeling of the three, painted his peasants with an entirely classical sincerity and restraint; he also showed a tender human sympathy that foreshadowed Chardin and Millet. One may with good reason compare the work of Caravaggio to certain austere, subtle still-lifes of Baugin and L. Linard, and it is further possible to speak of these artists in terms of a Parisian school of still-life painting in the time of Louis XIII.

## The first half of the 17th century

The calm simplicity of these realist painters is in striking contrast to the Baroque tendencies that were then beginning to appear in decorative and religious painting. When they returned from Italy, between 1625 and 1630, Claude Vignon, Jacques Blanchard, François Perrier, and especially Simon Vouet (the most talented of the group) had clearly benefited by their studies of the great Bolognese and Roman decorators. Their highly-colored paintings on the walls of Paris palaces and on church altarpieces—no doubt superficial but light and full of movement—are a fine tribute to their virtuosity.

These manifestations of a joyful Baroque style were short-lived. As early as 1640 Paris painters began to curb their flights of fantasy. Eustache Le Sueur, Laurent de La Hyre, Charles Lebrun and even Sébastien Bourdon, lured in their early days into following Vouet's example, adopted a more disciplined approach in their mature works: their compositions became more logical, their emotion more restrained, elegance occasionally giving way to austerity.

## Poussin

Meanwhile Nicolas Poussin, working in Rome, had evolved a more studied Classicism, the prestige of which encouraged his Paris colleagues into following new trends. Poussin was another painter who had felt the attraction of the Baroque style when young—his early works and his bacchanalia clearly show this. However, from about 1635 he deliberately toned down his sensuality; he began to construct his historical, mythological, and religious compositions according to a harmonious, arbitrarily-imposed rhythm. Even nature yielded to his single-minded determination to make an ordered spectacle of the universe and discover its underlying truths. Yet the profound lyricism that animates his last landscapes reveals clearly enough the emotion he had so resolutely mastered.

## Claude Lorraine

Less intellectual than Poussin, Claude Lorraine, another French painter working in Rome, created a different type of classical landscape. He began by studying Paul Bril and Elsheimer, but ended by following Poussin in his desire for clarity and immutable order. An over-all sense of balance governs his harbor scenes and views of the Roman countryside, transformed by an alternately bright or misty light into landscapes of a dream world. Here reality and convention are expressed in terms of poetry which, toward the end of the artist's life, broke out into pure fantasy. It was the 18th and 19th-century Romantics who were best able to appreciate his contribution to French art.

## The second half of the 17th century

Toward the middle of the 17th century, French painting had found, in Paris and in Rome, a subtle blend of free artistic sensibility and the laws of reason: a warm, emotional Classicism to which Philippe de Champaigne continued to adhere after early years spent under the influence of the Flemish Baroque style. In contrast to Bourdon's lively portraits, Champaigne's grave, motionless figures are the intense expression of his sitters' inner personalities, obtained by accurate analysis of their outward, physical features.

The year 1661 not only saw the start of Louis XIV's personal government, but also marked a major event in the history of art: Charles Lebrun was officially appointed First Painter to the King and for more than 20 years supervised a national and somewhat autocratic policy of art. As director of works he organized whole teams of painters, artists, and craftsmen at Versailles and other royal palaces; he supplied models for sculptors—even for architects—and cartoons for the tapestry weavers at the Gobelins workshops. He was well equipped for such a task by his training under Vouet, Poussin, and the Roman school, as well as by his important decorative works in the Hôtel Lambert and the Château de Vaux. He discharged his duties with personal authority, a sense of grandeur (though he was also guilty of pomposity), and a monumental scale of order in all things that synchronized perfectly with the king's own ambitions. The Hall of Mirrors at Versailles represents the most brilliant example of a style that the Academy, for many years afterward, sought to promote in historical painting.

## The "Rubenist" reaction

Lebrun's influence in creating a lofty but conventional style of painting was, however, challenged by other trends as early as 1680. Opposition to it came from the fashionable portraitist Pierre Mignard and from the "Rubenists" with their disregard for Lebrun's doctrine. In fact the "Rubenist" movement was more than a mere academic squabble. It went beyond plain admiration for the great Flemish painter; it was the concrete expression of a desire to restore to painting the rich colors and the quality of execution that the followers of Poussin had sacrificed for the sake of drawing and composition. Even amongst the Versailles group the Flemish painter van der Meulen, and Monnoyer, and Parrocel in his battle paintings, infringed the orthodox classical rules of Lebrun's collaborators. La Fosse, who, together with Coypel and Jouvenet, was the best representative of the Grand Manner at the end of the 17th century, was also one of these rebels. The vaulted roof in the chapel at Versailles, painted by all three of them in 1708, marks the official triumph of a new Baroque style, strongly influenced by the Roman illusionists. In some of their easel paintings La Fosse and Coypel even anticipated the lightness of the Rococo style. The style of Rigaud and Largillierre, as seen in their portrait paintings, and that of Desportes in his still-lifes, combined the theories of Jouvenet and La Fosse. A warmth of execution that owed much to the influence of the Netherlands, lavish decoration, and direct observation of nature—these are the hallmarks of a style that served as one of the sources of 18th-century art.

## Watteau

The "Rubenist" reaction against Academism eventually found in Antoine Watteau a champion with enough lyrical imagination to shine through his technical virtuosity. He painted in a tense, vigorous style with warm, vibrant tones; he was also the poet of his own enchanted world where melancholy was mingled with irony, where dreams were allied to sensuality, and fantasy to tender, uneasy intimations of reality. Although Watteau died young in 1721, he exercised a great influence both in France and abroad. To him 18th-century painting owes much of its grace and charm, despite the fact that the *fêtes galantes* painters, his imitators Jean Baptiste Pater and Nicolas Lancret, were blind to his lyricism and never succeeded in matching his subtle union of figures and landscape surrounded by glowing light—a union to which he alone held the secret.

## The coming of Rococo

Under Louis XV the flowering of a graceful school of painting, aimed at pleasing a new clientele of enlightened art-lovers, became increasingly evident. It was light, even frivolous, and its purpose was to afford an agreeable complement to Rococo boudoir and salon decor. The great historical paintings were quite out of place in these surroundings, and when they attempted them, a Coypel, a Carle van Loo or a Natoire remain meaningless or appear ridiculous. De Troy also gives of his best in scenes of manners or in rough sketches. Lemoyne and Restout alone undoubtedly knew differing methods of animating their vast compositions with a real Baroque breath of inspiration.

This worldly painting found its most brilliant exponent in François Boucher. A born "decorator," he composed his comic opera pastorals and gallant mythological scenes with a true understanding of the arabesques that married the curves and counter-curves peculiar to the Rococo style. Fashionable portrait painters in the first half of the century strove above all to please. Instead of pursuing a profound truth, they concentrated on charming decorative detail, as did Nattier, on fleeting vivacity of expression, as did Maurice Quentin de Latour, or on technical *brio*, as did Perronneau.

## Chardin

Chardin, the most penetrating observer of the century, was one of the few, in that era of artificiality and perpetual festivity, to observe and paint the plain truth. Another was Oudry, who depicted still-lifes and animals with a true-to-life accuracy learned from the Netherlanders. However, decoration always played an important part in Oudry's work, whereas Chardin painted objects and beings as they really appeared to him, concentrating only on the plasticity of form. His mastery of tonal values and lighting, combined with his sure handling, enabled him to produce the illusion of texture. At the same time his unerring instinct for group composition gave even his simplest still-lifes and domestic scenes a noble, monumental architecture and a gravity intensified by quiet emotion.

## Landscape painting in the 18th century

Like decorative painting and portraiture, 18th-century landscape painting was for a long time subject to the laws of an agreeable convention. In his marine views and paintings of French ports, Joseph Vernet rarely depicted his direct impressions of any given view. Hubert Robert, who followed in Vernet's footsteps, while adapting his scenes for purely decorative purposes, showed a more modern underlying sentiment. He took his inspiration from Giovanni Pannini, contrasting ancient classical ruins with scenes from daily life in an often melancholic, whimsical manner that still did not hinder his realistic observations of light and nature. In some of the Paris views Robert painted after his return from Italy in 1765, and even more so in the Île-de-France landscapes of Louis Moreau the Elder, there is a genuine feeling for landscape that anticipates the 19th century.

## Fragonard and Greuze

The most outstanding personality of the second half of the 18th century—Fragonard—also felt himself drawn to Italy. The revelation of a picturesque natural scene suffused with a warm glow of light, combined with what he had learned from Watteau, Boucher, and Rembrandt, was a major factor in his artistic development, and he emerged as a highly individual artist whose inspiration was expressed in terms of an exceptionally brilliant technique. His landscapes, his portraits, his gallant or domestic scenes, are all executed with tremendous high spirits and flashes of spontaneity. To keep in line with contemporary taste, Fragonard occasionally painted certain fashionable moralizing and sentimental subjects; yet he lost none of his technical virtuosity in the process. By about 1755 a reaction had already set in against over-frivolous painting. There emerged a school of painting based on sentiment and virtue; it found a willing exponent in Jean Baptiste Greuze—an expert at stirring the hearts of "sensitive souls." Yet although his subjects were often insipid or ambiguous, Greuze redeemed himself by the very real artistic gifts that shone forth in his portraits.

The reaction against excessive artificiality and fashionable charm was just as evident in portraiture and historical painting. It is true that some portrait painters did continue Nattier's vein of flattery, for instance Drouais and Madame Lebrun, but there were others like Tocqué and Duplessis who strove, often sincerely and always with great technical competence, for a more genuine simplicity and truth to life.

Historical painting returned to the Grand Manner. Ever since the middle of the century official policy had encouraged allegorical or historical works that exalted virtue and steadfast morality. In Rome, Subleyras had already produced a warm nobility of style which directly foreshadowed the new international movement known as Neoclassicism. Neoclassicism, which originated in Rome out of a renewed passion for antiquity and ideal beauty, was first seen in French art in 1760 in the "Pompeian" style of Joseph Marie Vien, but it was not until 20 years later that it found in David a painter capable of launching it as a fashion to be followed seriously.

## David

With his *Oath of the Horatii*, 1784 (p. 137), David at last provided what a whole generation had been waiting for. Until 1815 he continued to illustrate the fervor of the Revolution and the glory of Imperial Rome in both his contemporary and ancient classical works. In these paintings Naturalism, as in *The Death of Marat*, and heroic exaltation never obscured his classical harmony of composition. His rigid control of emotion sometimes made his paintings appear exceedingly cold. However, he could not entirely suppress his deep-rooted instincts as a painter and realist; not only was he an excellent portrait painter, but he succeeded in balancing grandeur and realism with a vigor that his numerous pupils failed to achieve. Nowadays Girodet, Gérard, and Guérin appeal to us less for their antiquarian or historical paintings than for their portraits and sketches. Similarly, the glossy perfection of the landscapes of Valenciennes or Bidault appeals to modern taste less than their oil sketches made on the spot in the Italian country-side: they already anticipated the poetry of Corot's works.

As was the case with Lebrun, David's dictatorship had

a less stultifying effect than has sometimes been thought. Genre painting (realistic painting of scenes taken from daily life) was largely an imitation of the 17th-century meticulous Dutch naturalism. Georges Michel, on the other hand, used the same ingredients to achieve the spirited style of his moving, tormented landscapes. When Pierre Paul Prud'hon turned to the fashionable classical themes, he always interpreted them with a refinement and voluptuous grace that harked back to the 18th century; his portraits were already beginning to be affected by a dreamy, pre-Romantic languor. He showed his hostility to the impersonal, arid character of Neoclassicism equally in his return to the hazy *sfumato* technique of Leonardo and Correggio.

Even among the ranks of the Neoclassicists, dissension could be detected. Antoine Gros, for instance, flouted Academism by the epic sense of reality that animated his major works glorifying the imperial army. With its love of movement, life, and space, its free handling and warm colors, his art is one of the vital sources of Romanticism.

### Ingres

Ingres, however, is a more ambiguous personality. He was a pupil of David and an admirer of Raphael; all his life he propounded the doctrine of ideal beauty and orthodox Classicism, never deviating from his inflexible attitude even when Romanticism rose to favor. Yet a closer look at his masterpieces shows that his Classicism is anything but orthodox, his idealism often tinged with extravagance. In his most original works, harmony and verisimilitude are always sacrificed in favor of sinuous line. This occasionally brings its reward in a most unusual effect. His preciosity also leads him to adopt arbitrary color schemes. A romantic by virtue of his "Gothic" or Oriental subjects, he reveals himself, even in his most ostensibly classical nude studies or portraits, a pure Mannerist, a poet of rare and exotic things—a "Chinese painter lost... amid the ruins of Athens," as a contemporary aptly described him.

### The Romantic movement

Heralded by Gros, the Romantic movement burst into public notice at the Salon of 1819, where Théodore Géricault exhibited *The Raft of the Medusa* (p. 147). The hostility aroused by this masterpiece marked the prelude to repeated scandals that punctuated the history of 19th-century painting. The rift between progressive art and public opinion, which was at its widest about 1870 at the end of the Second Empire, was already apparent when the Romantic battle was being waged. From then onward the great artists were always more or less lone figures, standing on the fringe of official art. At the same time the difficulties of winning recognition encouraged painters to join forces and rally for battle under the same flag. The evolution of great art is seen during the course of the century as a succession of pitched battles and different movements reacting against each other, each movement countering the previous one as soon as the first had been accepted and assimilated into Academism.

Because of his vitality, his obsession with death, and, from the technical angle, his free handling, Géricault was undoubtedly a Romantic. He was, however, susceptible to the classical system of order; and this gave his work a solidity and plasticity that was accentuated by his concern for the realities of contemporary life. Such emphasis on life "in the raw" was rare among the other Romantics. For them painting was an escape from the present: an escape in time, which led them back to the Middle Ages, where they could find countless strange, picturesque scenes; an escape into fantasy and nostalgia, encouraging them for example to illustrate the Napoleonic legend; an escape in terms of space and distance, seeking the exotic luxury of the unknown through their studies of the Orient. Even in their landscapes the Romantics showed a preference for strange, desolate places and unusual aspects of nature.

### Delacroix

Although there is still evidence of some Classicism in his works, Delacroix succeeded in giving a pictorial form to the great Romantic dream-world. He took his lead from Géricault and the English painters, and—with Rubens and the Venetians in mind—recreated a heroic Grand Manner. He had no qualms about working on a gigantic scale; in fact he welcomed the opportunity to devise vast murals in the Chamber of Deputies, the Senate, and the Church of St. Sulpice. He also revived the great themes of old, portraying sensual pleasure, suffering, violence, luxury, fervor, and dignity; he drew on legend and literature as well as on memories of his travels in Morocco that had opened up to him the magic of the Islamic world. All these sources furnished him with themes or anecdotes which, by his intense meditation on contemporary life and history, he was able to raise to the level of universal allegory. Yet this intellectual approach was always expressed in purely pictorial terms. Delacroix remained above all else a painter whose perpetual experiments with color and technique gave his canvases and murals the quivering intensity of life itself.

Limited as they were by their over-literary approach, the imaginative powers of the other Romantic historical painters were not always served by a pictorial skill as exceptional as that of Delacroix. The style of Horace Vernet remained in the academic mold; others revealed their true talent most of all in their sketches. Of the "orientalists," Decamps is more appreciated today for his mastery of movement and light than for his conventional exoticism. Of the other minor anecdotal or historical masters there remain only the period charm and the lively imagination of their arresting, spirited sketches.

Accepted both by the general public and in official circles, the Romantic school enjoyed a prestige that continued throughout the Second Empire. Its mixture of classical and realist elements often resulted in a sterile eclecticism. However, Couture and Ribot above all merit fame and have on the whole been too hastily dismissed by modern critics.

Théodore Chassériau, however, surpassed them all for his warmth of feeling. Although a pupil of Ingres, he took most of his subjects from Delacroix and the memory of his travels in Algeria. He made a skillful synthesis of his first master's graphic stylization and his second master's brilliant colors and lyrical content. When in the course of time he became a teacher himself, he provided Pierre Puvis de Chavannes with an example of serene harmony that he followed in his vast mural decorations. Gustave Moreau pursued Chassériau's vague, exotic, magical fantasies until late in the century.

## Corot

Even before the Realist movement had, toward the middle of the century, given a new turn to progressive painting, Corot, a solitary figure far removed from all literary trends, succeeded without publicity or scandal in achieving straightforward observations of nature. Though modern taste may dismiss the studio landscapes he painted for the Salon and the landscapes that success led him to paint with too much facility, it is now possible to discern in his Italian or French provincial views— painted actually on the spot—a freshness of light and a mastery of tonal value that make him one of the greatest French landscape painters to precede Cézanne. His unerring instinct for composition and the exactness of each note of color give his paintings, and even his simple oil sketches, a broad unity that never hinders the expression of his emotion. By his fresh direct observation of light and his unconventional technique, Corot took landscape painting to the threshold of Impressionism.

## The evolution of landscape painting

While Corot was making his experiments, other 19th-century landscape painters passed through three distinct stages of development, the last of which foreshadowed the Impressionist revolution. The earliest stage, from about 1830 to 1835, was characterized by a romantic lyricism. Paul Huet, Eugène Isabey and, in their early works, Théodore Rousseau and Jules Dupré, aimed at dramatic effects; their scenes were natural, but full of life and movement. Strongly influenced by new developments in England, they used brushwork that was either vigorous or light, but always rapid and sweeping. In the second period—about 1850—a group of painters led by Rousseau and including, among others, Diaz de la Peña, Dupré, and Troyon, became established at Barbizon in the forest of Fontainebleau. These landscape painters, who were more realistic than the Romantics (the Dutch masters had had some influence here), devoted their attention mostly to the forest and plain. Their descriptive works, which were intended to be faithulf representations of peasant life and free from all literary devices, have an intimate yet universal atmosphere about them. Rousseau in particular, concerned with making an exact transcription of the scene, developed an elaborate, precise technique. After 1860 the landscape painters again changed their outlook. Chintreuil, Harpignies and above all Daubigny often painted sky and water, approaching the subject with an objectivity which set aside all emotion. They whole-heartedly studied the effects of light and observed the changing magic of its reflections. The way now lay open for Jongkind and Boudin.

## Realism

Millet was the best representative of the realist Barbizon group that, about 1850, set up in violent opposition to official Academism and waning Romanticism. Millet withdrew into the country with the object of portraying different aspects of peasant life—the dignity and poetry inherent in field and farm labor. His grasp of the old masters' techniques enabled him to give style to the sincerity of his portrayal. His is a virile, synthetic manner aimed at evoking a vision of harmony and depth, though it is often spoiled by thick, heavy coloring. Millet remained essentially a classical artist, another Poussin painting Le Nain subjects.

Daumier, on the other hand, portraying alternately the poverty and the absurdities of his times, showed a verve, passion, and dynamic energy that stemmed from the Baroque style. His realism is seen in the accuracy with which he captures a lawyer's gesture or a washerwoman's silhouette, but, cruel or tender, his is the truth of a visionary. In his trenchant way he accentuated form and heightened dramatic contrasts of light and shadow. In short, what is now called Expressionism is seen in embryo form in Daumier's paintings.

To his contemporaries Courbet was the arch-champion of Realism—more so than Millet and Daumier, who were too modest and self-effacing. His aggressive temperament, moreover, fitted him admirably for this role. Courbet's realism was a complete rejection of any form of idealism; it demanded, moreover, the portrayal of subjects that were sometimes sordid and depressing. For Courbet it was not an artist's job to indulge in imagination; he should "interpret the manners, the ideas, the appearances of his times" and be prepared to denounce poverty and political scandal. Fortunately Courbet was only seldom successful in fulfilling this artistic function of appealing to his contemporaries' social conscience. He painted his native Jura, and bright, clear seascapes, animals, fruit, his friends, self-portraits, and strong, healthy nudes. On the occasions when he set out to champion a cause, his instinct as a painter dominated his humanitarian principles. Courbet, self-taught by studying old masters, was an incomparable craftsman with a natural aptitude for composition. He laid on paint as if his palette knife were a trowel, producing effects that ranged from the extremely powerful to the extremely delicate. He put moral overtones into his more elaborate compositions and gave the simpler ones a monumental grandeur that was ultimately worthy to succeed the heroic Grand Manner he had wanted to abolish.

Corot, Millet, Daumier, Courbet and the others, with their refusal to accept the outworn assumptions of the Academists, their opposition to the Classical and Romantic views of painting, and their fresh, direct observation of nature, paved the way for the advent of Impressionism, the next great phase in European art.

# Biographies

# SOME BOOKS FOR FURTHER READING

A. Blunt, *The French Drawings in the Collection of His Majesty the King at Windsor Castle*, Oxford and London, 1945.

G. Ring, *A Century of French Painting*, 1400-1500, London, 1949.

A. Blunt, *Art and Architecture in France*, 1500-1700, London (Pelican History of Art) 1953.

J. Leymarie, *The Nineteenth Century*, Vol. 3, French Painting, Geneva, 1962.

A. Chatelet and J. Thuillier, *From Fouquet to Poussin*, Vol. 1, French Painting, Geneva, 1963.

A. Chatelet and J. Thuillier, *From Le Nain to Fragonard*, Vol. 2, French Painting, Geneva, 1964.

SEE ALSO UNDER THE INDIVIDUAL BIOGRAPHIES

# ANTOINE LOUIS BARYE 1796-1875

*A romantic animal sculptor*

Son of a Paris goldsmith, Antoine Louis Barye fought with Napoleon's army from 1812 to 1814, and began to study sculpture in 1816. After several unsuccessful attempts at the Prix de Rome, he began in 1823 to work for the goldsmith Fauconnier, modeling the animals in the Jardin des Plantes in Paris. He devoted himself almost entirely to animal sculpture, and in the Paris Salon of 1833 his *Lion Crushing a Serpent* won wide acclaim.

In spite of this, animal sculpture was considered an inferior genre, and was not recognized by the Academy. In 1848 Barye was declared bankrupt, but was appointed Keeper of the Casts at the Louvre. This helped him temporarily, and in 1854 a post as Professor of Zoological Drawing at the Natural History Museum in Paris set him free from immediate financial worries.

Between 1854 and 1860 Barye worked on sculptural decorations for the new buildings of the Louvre, including a relief of *Napoleon III Dominating History and the Arts*, which formed a pediment of the Pavillon de l'Horloge. In 1865 he completed his last major work, an equestrian statue of Napoleon I, for Ajaccio, Corsica, Bonaparte's birthplace. He died in 1875.

On the whole, however, Barye preferred animal subjects, particularly the large carnivores, jaguars, tigers, and lions, which in his work make an interesting parallel to the animal paintings of Delacroix. Although Barye's sculptures were much admired during his lifetime, his choice of subject prevented the highest official recognition. He was also a gifted draftsman, painter, and watercolorist.

A Horse
*London, Private Collection, et al.*

BARYE

**HIS WORKS INCLUDE**

Lion Crushing a Serpent
(bronze) 1832
*Paris, Louvre, et al.*
Wolf and Deer (plaster and wax) 1843
*Paris, Louvre*
Seated Lion (plaster model) 1847
*Paris, Louvre*
Portrait of the Artist's Daughter
(painting)
*Paris, Louvre*

**See also page 210**

---

# BAUGIN active about 1630

*A realistic still-life painter*

Nothing certain is known about the life of Baugin, and only one of his canvases is dated—*Books and Papers by Candlelight* of 1630. His activity seems to have been centered on a school of still-life painters that grew up in the Saint-Germain-des-Prés quarter of Paris at the beginning of the 17th century.

Baugin's work is known from three signed canvases, one of which is the dated painting mentioned above. The other two are entitled *The Five Senses*, a still-life of objects symbolizing each of the senses, and *The Dessert of Wafers*. The three works are all austere in color and restrained in composition. Baugin signed his paintings with his surname only; he is not to be confused with his Parisian namesake, Lubin Baugin, an imitator of Bolognese painters and Guido Reni.

The Dessert of Wafers
*Paris, Louvre*

**HIS WORKS INCLUDE**

Books and Papers by Candlelight, 1630
*Rome, Spada Gal.*
The Five Senses
*Paris, Louvre*

**See also page 113**

The Three Marys
*London, B. M., et al.*

# JACQUES BELLANGE

active 1600-1617

*A highly imaginative Mannerist artist and engraver*

Although Jacques Bellange is recorded as being in Nancy between 1600 and 1617, engaged on painting portraits, decorating rooms in the ducal palace, and helping in the preparation of court festivities, little is known of his life. Nothing of his work survives except a number of drawings and engravings.

The style of his work suggests that Bellange visited Rome in the last decade of the 16th century, and was familiar with the painting of Federico (Baroccio) Barocci and his followers. His etchings represent the final stage of an aspect of Mannerism that began with Parmigianino and that expressed a particular type of religious emotion, an effect obtained through the introduction of forms of great elegance and elongation. This Mannerist strain was combined with the knowledge of various Flemish, Dutch, and German engravings. Bellange used this repertoire of influences to create varied effects of surprise and mystery.

Bellange's most important works appear to have been religious in character. He also produced some scenes of contemporary life that provide a contrast to his normally elegant figures. He died in 1617.

**HIS WORKS INCLUDE**

The Annunciation (etching)
*London, B. M., et al.*

The Adoration of the Magi (etching)
*Paris, Louvre, et al.*

A Group of Women (pen drawing)
*Paris, Louvre*

**See also page 169**

---

The Communion and
Martyrdom of St. Denis
(detail) about 1416
*Paris, Louvre*

**See also page 88**

# HENRI BELLECHOSE

active 1400 - about 1444

*A painter of the Burgundian court*

Little is known of the life of Henri Bellechose, who was a Flemish court painter to the dukes of Burgundy. He was born in Brabant, and he succeeded Jean Malouel at the Burgundian court. Between 1416 and 1425 he worked for John the Fearless and later for Philip the Good, at the Chartreuse de Champmol outside Dijon, in the palace of Dijon, and in other ducal castles. In 1398 Jean Malouel was commissioned to paint five altarpieces for the Chartreuse. He does not appear to have completed this commission, however, and *The Communion and Martyrdom of St. Denis*, though part of Malouel's commission, is believed to be entirely by Bellechose.

## JACQUES BLANCHARD

1600-1638

*A painter somewhat optimistically called by his contemporaries "The Titian of France"*

Jacques Blanchard was brought up and trained in the Mannerist tradition by his uncle, the painter Nicolas Bollery. In 1620 he traveled from Paris to Lyons, where he worked for a time under Horace Le Blanc. He later went to Rome and to Venice, where he spent two years, studying Veronese in particular. In 1628 Blanchard returned to Paris, stopping at Turin and Lyons.

In Paris Blanchard enjoyed some success as a painter of small religious and mythological subjects, in which the cool colors of Veronese are much in evidence. The sentiment of his work—for instance, *Charity*, which exists in many versions—tends to be delicate, sometimes over delicate.

Blanchard was also a sensitive and successful portrait painter.

A Bacchanal
*Nancy, Mus. des B-A.*

HIS WORKS INCLUDE
Cimon and Ephigène
*Paris, Louvre*

**See also page 107**

---

## EDMÉ BOUCHARDON

1698-1762

*A successful sculptor who worked for Louis XV*

Edmé Bouchardon was born in Chaumont on May 29, 1698. He was the son of a sculptor, and went into his father's studio as a pupil in about 1715, remaining there until 1721. He then went to Paris and became the pupil of Guillaume Coustou I. He won the first prize for sculpture at the Academy school in 1722. A year later he received a grant, and went to Rome. Bouchardon spent nine years in Italy, where he made numerous copies of antique sculpture, and became well known for his work, particularly for his portrait busts. However, the Duke of Antin, who was superintendent of the king's buildings, forced him to return to Paris in 1732.

Here Bouchardon was given an apartment in the Louvre, and he carried out many commissions for the king, including a statue of Louis XIV for the Cathedral of Notre Dame, and the *Fountain of Neptune* at Versailles. In 1736 he succeeded Jean Chaufourrier as the designer for the Academy of Inscriptions and Belles-Lettres, for which he made several medals during the reign of Louis XV. He was also commissioned to make a fountain for the rue de Grenelle, Faubourg Saint-Germain, his most successful work, and the equestrian statue of Louis XV, which was placed in the Place Louis XV (now the Place de la Concorde) but was destroyed in the Revolution. Bouchardon was admitted to the Royal Academy of Painting and Sculpture in 1745, following the execution of a statuette of *Christ Leaning on His Cross*. A year later he was made a professor.

In his later life he sculpted decorations for the Church of St. Sulpice. His style here as in his earlier works shows that he depended greatly on antique patterns,

Sleeping Faun (detail) 1732
*Paris, Louvre*

HIS WORKS INCLUDE

Pope Clement XII, 1730
*Florence, Corsini Gall.*

Christ Leaning on His Cross, 1745
*Paris, Louvre*

Cupid with his Bow, about 1750
*Paris, Louvre*

**See also page 204**

*Bouchardon* and his work generally marks a return to Classicism. He made numerous drawings, not only studies for sculpture, but portraits, mythological subjects, ornamented frontispieces, and engravings, of which the best known are the *Cries of Paris*, designed for the Comte de Caylus and published from 1737 to 1746. Bouchardon died on July 27, 1762.

LUNDBERG
Portrait of François Boucher
*Paris, Louvre*

## FRANÇOIS BOUCHER

1703-1770

*One of the most typical and successful of Rococo decorative painters*

François Boucher's father was an embroidery designer, and as a boy the artist worked at this trade. When the scope of his talent became evident he was apprenticed to the engraver Laurent Cars, and afterwards became a pupil of François Le Moyne, who was responsible for the Salon d'Hercule at Versailles. He was also influenced by Watteau, whose work he engraved.

In 1723 Boucher won the Prix de Rome, but jealousy within the Academy curtailed his privileges. When he did make the journey to Rome in 1727, it was not on the proceeds of this prize, but with a private collector. He stayed in Italy until 1731, where he was greatly impressed by the work of the illusionist Baroque painters, Francesco Trevisani, Benedetto Luti, but above all by Correggio. On his return to Paris he made a living as an etcher and book illustrator.

In 1734 Boucher became a member of the Academy, and thereafter success

The Triumph of Venus, 1740
*Stockholm, Nationalmus.*

The Visit of Venus to Vulcan
(detail) 1754  *London, Wallace Coll.*

20

came quickly. Madame de Pompadour, Louis XV's mistress, a witty, intelligent and powerful woman, made him her friend and faithful servant. A man of great energy and spontaneity, Boucher produced for her and her circle endless decorations, pictures, and designs for everything from theater sets to dolls, fans, and snuff boxes. He was also much in demand as a portraitist, and painted Madame de Pompadour seven times. Fragonard was one of his pupils.

In spite of his success, Boucher had his detractors. Diderot, the French philosopher, said of his work that it was "nothing but young women with rouged, simpering faces!" The English artist Reynolds visited Boucher and was appalled to find him working without a model. He reported that Boucher "said, when he was young, studying his art, he found it necessary to use models, but he had left them off for many years."

Boucher was made Director of the Academy in 1765. A rich and successful man, happily married, and the owner of a valuable collection of objets d'art, he was troubled only by a feeling that his popularity was waning. Whether this feeling was justified or not, both the demand for his work and his vitality to meet it were maintained until his death in 1770.

*C. M. Bearn   A Court Painter and his Circles: François Boucher   London, 1913*

## HIS WORKS INCLUDE
Renaud and Armide, 1734
*Paris, Louvre*

Le Déjeuner, 1739
*Paris, Louvre*

Diana Resting after the Bath, 1742
*Paris, Louvre*

The Hermit, 1742
*Leningrad, Hermitage*

Pan and Syrinx, 1759
*London, N. G.*

The Mill, late work
*Orléans, Mus. des B-A.*

**See also pages 127, 128, 180**

---

## SÉBASTIEN BOURDON                                    1616-1671

*A competent but not pre-eminent painter of history pieces, portraits, and landscapes*

Sébastien Bourdon was born in Montpellier in 1616, but at the age of seven he was taken to Paris. In about 1634 he went to Rome, where he remained for three years perfecting his style in imitation of the Bambocciati (painters of low-life subjects in the style of Bamboccia) and Giovanni Castiglione. Although able to paint in any style, he never evolved a manner of his own. It is much more to Claude Lorraine's credit than to Bourdon's that in about 1634 Bourdon found it worthwhile to pass off one of his own paintings as the work of Claude.

From 1637 Bourdon was again in Paris, continuing to work in an Italianate manner. In 1643 he painted an ambitious Baroque piece entitled *The Martyrdom of St. Peter*. In 1652 Bourdon went to Sweden at the invitation of Queen Christina, and there painted many portraits of the queen and her court. On her abdication in 1654 he returned to Paris, where he continued to enjoy great success as a portrait painter. These were the most accomplished of his works. His later style became increasingly restrained and Poussinesque, though he added to it a certain sweet charm that appealed to his public. It is in his later works, however, that Bourdon achieved a more personal manner.

The Martyrdom of St. Peter, 1643
*Paris, Notre Dame*

## HIS WORKS INCLUDE
The Kiln
*Munich, Alte Pin.*

Portrait of Christina of Sweden, about 1652
*Madrid, Prado*

**See also page 111**

Scene from The Miseries of War
(detail) 1633
*London, B. M., et al.*

# JACQUES CALLOT

1592/3-1635

*An outstanding engraver*

Jacques Callot was born in 1592 or 1593 in Nancy, where his father was King-at-Arms to Duke Charles III. In 1607 Jacques was apprenticed to Demange Crocq, a local goldsmith. He left France some time between 1608 and 1611, and joined the French engraver Philippe Thomassin in Rome. During this period he learned the various techniques of engraving, and came into contact with the late Mannerist works to be seen in Roman churches.

Towards the end of 1611 Callot visited Florence, where he became attached to the ducal court of Cosimo II. He quickly established his reputation, and produced numerous series of plates depicting court festivities. In 1612 he began a series that recorded the ceremonies in memory of the death of the Queen of Spain, and soon afterwards he began a number of plates celebrating the life of Ferdinand of Tuscany.

Callot's work not only reflects the Mannerist devices current in his day, and the influence of engravings by Bosch and Bruegel, but also an acute observation of nature. Many of his characters, such as those in *The Two Pantaloons*, derived from the Commedia dell'Arte and from court pageantry. He loved to depict beggars and grotesquely deformed people in contrast with the aristocratic elegance of the court. His career in Italy came to an end when the Grand Duke died in 1621, and his pension was canceled.

Callot returned to Nancy, where he worked under the patronage of Charles of Lorraine. He carried on various types of etching, and in 1622 produced the finest of his studies in his grotesque manner, *The Gypsies*. In 1627 he engraved pictures of the celebrations held in honor of the exiled Duchess of Longueville. It was during this period that a slight change in his style occurred, and he began to take an interest in landscape for its own sake. In these works motifs from the engravings of Bruegel reveal the influence of the Netherlandish Mannerist tradition.

After his return to Nancy, Callot produced several series of religious etchings.

Landscape with Standing Figure
(detail)  *London, B. M.*

The Agony in the Garden, 1625
*Chatsworth, England, Trustees of the Chatsworth Settlement*

22

These contain many elements of Mannerism, using devices of scale and lighting to give a sense of drama and heightened emotion to the whole. About 1625 he went to Brussels to carry out a commission for the Infanta Clara Eugenia, the huge series of *The Siege of Breda*. About 1629 he was invited to Paris by Richelieu to commemorate the capture of La Rochelle in a series of engravings. Two years later Callot returned to Nancy, and continued his work. In 1633 Richelieu invaded Lorraine, and in the same year the artist etched his series, *The Miseries of War*, in which the atrocities of war are observed with a terrifying detachment. He died two years afterwards.

Callot was one of the greatest of etchers, and in his work can be found elements that recur in Rococo art.

Scene from The Miseries of War, 1633
*London, B. M., et al.*

**HIS WORKS INCLUDE**

The Two Pantaloons (etching) 1616
*London, B. M., et al.*

Florentine Fête (etching) 1619
*London, B. M., et al.*

The Gypsies (etching) 1622
*London, B. M., et al.*

The Siege of Breda (etching)
about 1628
*London, B. M., et al.*

The Siege of La Rochelle (etching)
about 1629
*London, B. M., et al.*

The Temptation of St. Anthony
(drawing) about 1635
*Florenze, Uffizi*

The Martyrdom of St. Sebastian
(charcoal and wash)
*London, V. and A.*

**See also page 171**

---

## ANTOINE CARON                                     about 1520 - about 1600

*One of the most notable painters of the School of Fontainebleau*

Antoine Caron is first recorded as working under Primaticcio on decorations at Fontainebleau; these were executed some time before 1550. Little is known about his life, but there is evidence that he was closely connected with the Catholic League. Certainly he later became painter to Catherine de' Medici, and he was a friend of the poet and Catholic apologist Louis of Orléans.

In common with other members of the School of Fontainebleau, Caron was influenced both by the Italian painters at the French court and by the current interest in Greek and Roman antiquity. Though his style was entirely personal, his elaborate architectural, almost theatrical, backgrounds show the culmination of these influences. The strange elongation of his figures was due to the example of Niccolò dell'Abbate, but in Caron's hands they became far more exaggerated and unrealistic.

Not many paintings can be attributed with any certainty to Caron. Those that can are mainly allegorical themes, fantastic scenes such as *Augustus and the Sibyl*, or compositions depicting massacres. Caron was also employed on the masques and decorations used in court festivities. He worked with some other court artists on a series of drawings dedicated to the glory of Henry II and Catherine de' Medici, which were also reproduced as tapestries. Caron's work is typical of the most sophisticated court Mannerism.

Augustus and the Sibyl
*Paris, Louvre*

**HIS WORKS INCLUDE**

The Massacres under the Triumvirate,
1566
*Paris, Louvre*

Illustrations for Houel's
"Histoire des Rois de France"
*Paris, Bibl. Nat.*

The Resurrection
*Beavais, Mus. des B-A.*

**See also page 167**

# JEAN BAPTISTE CARPEAUX 1827-1875

Self-portrait
*Valenciennes, Mus. des B-A.*

*A famous sculptor of the Second Empire*

Jean Baptiste Carpeaux was born in Valenciennes on May 11, 1827, and there received his early training. In 1842 he went to Paris, where he studied under the leading Romantic sculptor, François Rude. With his sculpture *Hector*, Carpeaux won the Prix de Rome, and he was able to spend some years in Italy. Here he was greatly impressed by Michelangelo's *Last Judgment*, and by reading Dante's "Inferno". His *Ugolino and his Starving Sons*, 1857-1861, is a reflection of this interest, and an exception among his works in its realism.

Although he met with opposition from the more conservative sections of Paris society, Carpeaux was soon successful. His first important commission was for decorations on the Pavillon de Flore in the Tuileries, where between 1863 and 1866 he carried out decorations on the pediment and a relief of *Flora with Dancing Cupids*. The style of his sculpture is particularly lively, containing both Michelangelesque and sensual Rococo elements.

Carpeaux produced his most famous group, *The Dance*, in the years 1865 to 1869. This was designed to decorate the new Opera House in Paris, and created a great stir. The work, full of vitality and movement, is in keeping with the architecture.

Other important works by Carpeaux are the *Memorial to Watteau* in Valenciennes, begun in 1869 and completed by another hand after his death, and the figures of 1872 representing the *Four Continents* on the fountain in the Luxembourg Gardens. He also produced many accomplished portrait busts and paintings.

## HIS WORKS INCLUDE

Hector (marble) about 1845
*Paris, École des B-A.*

Imperial Prince with his Dog Nero
(marble) 1865
*Paris, Louvre*

The Ball at the Tuileries (oil) 1867
*Paris, Louvre*

The Dance, 1865-69
*Paris, Opera*

**See also page 210**

Mademoiselle Fiocre
*Paris, Louvre*

Ugolino and his Starving Sons, 1857-61
*Paris, Jardin des Tuileries*

Ugolino and his Starving Sons (detail) 1857-61
*Paris, Jardin des Tuileries*

# PHILIPPE DE CHAMPAIGNE 1602-1674

*A successful portrait painter*

Philippe de Champaigne was born in Brussels, where he was trained as a landscape painter. In 1621 he went to Paris and met Poussin, with whom he collaborated on the decorations of the Luxembourg Palace. After a short return visit to Brussels, he became in 1628 painter to the queen mother, Maria de' Medici. He gained the favor of Louis XIII and painted a portrait of the king being crowned by Victory against a background of La Rochelle, where the Protestants had been defeated shortly before. His triple portrait of Richelieu, the king's chief minister, resembles that by van Dyck of Charles I, but this is partly because both were painted for the same purpose, to be used as models for portrait busts. The more important influence on Champaigne is that of Rubens, but a Rubens rationalized and controlled, made acceptable to the intellectual temper of the French, through Champaigne's more lucid and cerebral manner, calmer poses, and strong cool color.

In 1643, Champaigne came into contact with the nuns of Port Royal, when both his daughters joined the convent. In common with many other serious men of his time, he was attracted by the severe and sincere doctrine of the Jansenists. The effect of their teaching is to be seen in all Champaigne's works after this date. He finally rejected the Baroque style, and his later works, often civic group portraits, attain real originality in their restrained poses and sober coloring. The masterpiece of this period is a votive picture painted in gratitude for his daughter's cure. She was attacked in 1660 by a paralysis which by the end of 1661 made her unable to walk. The prioress declared a *novena* in the hope that she might be cured, and at the end of the nine days she found herself suddenly able to walk. The painting shows the prioress kneeling beside the sick nun. It is simple and geometrically severe in its composition; the only touches of color are the two crimson crosses on the nuns' robes, and even one of these is partly obscured.

Champaigne was the best and most successful portrait painter of his day. He had many pupils and assistants in his studio in Paris, where he worked until his death.

Self-portrait (detail)
*Paris, Louvre*

*Phil de Champaigne.*

HIS WORKS INCLUDE

Louis XIII Crowned by Victory,
about 1629
*Paris, Louvre*

Triple Portrait of Cardinal Richelieu,
about 1635
*London, N. G.*

St. Joseph's Dream
*London, N. G*

Échevins of the City of Paris, 1648
*Paris, Louvre*

**See also page 110**

The Adoration of the Shepherds (detail)
*London, Wallace Coll.*

An Unknown Man, 1650
*Paris, Louvre*

*A painter of the scenes and objects of everyday domestic life*

Jean Baptiste Siméon Chardin was born in Paris on November 2, 1699, the son of a Paris cabinetmaker. From an early age he had to make his living, and at 18 he was a student of a painter of historical scenes, Pierre Jacques Cazes, whose works he copied. He continued with various jobs, including the restoration of frescoes at Fontainebleau, under the supervision of Carle van Loo. In 1728 Chardin sent several paintings to the open-air exhibition of young painters held annually in the Place Dauphine. Later the same year he was accepted as a member of the Academy. In his earlier period he painted still-lifes of simple domestic objects—kitchen utensils, fruit, and game.

During the 1730's Chardin's style matured, and he painted genre scenes, depicting the life of the people around him, including *Le Bénédicité* and *The Kitchen Maid*. Chardin continued to show his work at the Salon with great success. He attracted the attention of several collectors, and many of his paintings were known to the public through engravings. He did not look for lively scenes. His figures are caught in a moment of stillness—a child inspects her mother's embroidery or listens to her

Self-portrait, 1771
*Paris, Louvre*

**Chardin**

HIS WORKS INCLUDE

The Buffet, 1728
*Paris, Louvre*

The Kitchen Maid, about 1735
*Glasgow, Art Gall.*

The House of Cards, about 1741
*London, N. G.*

Basket of Peaches, 1768
*Paris, Louvre*

Portrait of Madame Chardin
(pastel) 1775
*Paris, Louvre*

**See also pages 124, 125, 126**

A Mother Working, about 1740
*Paris, Louvre*

The Young Schoolmistress
*London, N. G.*

advice, a woman back from the market rests her heavy bundle against the kitchen shelf. All are painted with the same attention to detail, infinitely subtle coloring, and fullness of volume that distinguish his still-lifes.

Chardin's health began to deteriorate as he advanced toward old age, and eventually he found his meticulous method of oil painting too difficult. In his last years he turned to pastels. This enabled him to produce far more quickly. His technique and his interest in the ordered composition of form remained the same.

In the 1775 Salon Chardin exhibited, alongside Maurice Quentin de Latour's far more fashionable pastels, his masterpieces in this medium, two self-portraits and a portrait of his wife. His popularity declined in the late 1770's, and he lost one of his powerful patrons, but he appears to have been able to ensure a regular income in his old age. Chardin was certainly the greatest master of still-life painting in the 18th century. In his ability to sense and portray the basic, underlying form of objects he is in some ways a forerunner of Cézanne.

B. Denvir  Chardin  New York, 1950

Still-life
*Stockholm, Nationalmus.*

---

## THÉODORE CHASSÉRIAU                    1819-1856

*A painter who mixed the classical and romantic styles*

The work of Théodore Chassériau, born in 1819, represents the only successful attempt to combine the classical influence of Ingres with the romantic vein of Delacroix. Chassériau's family were Creoles from Hispaniola who moved to Paris in 1822. Between 1830 and 1834 he worked in Ingres' studio, and his *Susanna* of 1839 and the *Venus Anadyomede* of the same year show Ingres' influence in their oval-faced, languid nudes. In *Christ in the Garden of Olives*, however, painted in 1840 for the Cathedral of St. Jean d'Angély, the composition and technique were inspired by Delacroix.

For the rest of his life Chassériau oscillated between the two leaders of French art. In 1832 and 1833 he painted frescoes in the Neoclassical tradition representing the life of St. Mary the Egyptian in the Church of St. Merri, Paris; later he painted allegorical compositions for the Cour des Comptes of the Palais d'Orsay. Some of these were destroyed by fire, but the remaining panels are preserved in the Louvre.

After sketching a party of Bedouins seen at Marseilles in 1836, Chassériau concentrated more and more on Arab themes. In 1844 he did a series of engraved illustrations of *Othello*, and, after a voyage to Algeria in 1846, the series *The Caliph of Constantine*. In 1853 he painted his famous *Tepidarium*, Louvre, Paris, which depicts nudes in a vaguely Eastern setting. Like Ingres he excelled in portraits of women; he painted a double portrait of his two sisters Adèle and Aline in 1843. He also made many lively pencil drawings of them and of his beloved Alice Ozy. Although he died at an early age, in 1856, Chassériau's creative powers, at their greatest in his early works, had already largely evaporated.

Father Lacordaire
*Paris, Louvre*

### HIS WORKS INCLUDE

Susanna and the Elders, 1839
*Paris, Louvre*

Venus Anadyomede, 1839
*Paris, Louvre*

Decorations for the Cour des Comptes, 1848
*Paris, Louvre*

Alice Ozy, 1850
*Avignon, Mus. Calvet*

**See also pages 159, 192**

# CLAUDE GELLÉE or LORRAINE

*The originator of a type of poetic landscape that has been much copied*

The landscape painter Claude Gellée is best known as Claude Lorraine, the name deriving from the district of his birth. Orphaned at the age of 12, he left home and traveled to Rome to work as a pastry-cook. He was engaged in the household of the landscape painter Agostino Tassi, and he contrived to change his status from cook to apprentice. From 1618 to 1620 he was probably in Naples, the coastline of which appears constantly in his work. He returned to Nancy in 1625, but by 1627 was back in Rome.

R. COLLIN
Portrait of Claude Lorraine
*Paris, Bibl. Nat.*

Ascanius and the Stag, 1682
*Oxford, Ashmolean*

Landscape: View of the Campagna (watercolor)
*London, B. M.*

## HIS WORKS INCLUDE

A Harbor at Sunset, 1639
*Paris, Louvre*

View of Tivoli, 1640-45
*Grenoble, Mus.*

The Arrival of Cleopatra at Tarsus,
about 1645
*Paris, Louvre*

The Siege of La Rochelle, 1651
*Paris, Louvre*

Christ at Emmaus, 1652
*Leningrad, Hermitage*

David at the Cave of Adullam, 1658
*London, N. G.*

Landscape with Psyche and the
Palace of Amor, 1664
*Wantage, England, coll. Mr. C. L. Lloyd*

Aeneas Hunting in Libya, 1672
*Brussels, Mus. Royaux des B-A.*

Aeneas at Delos, 1672
*London, N. G.*

Liber Veritatis (drawings)
*London, B. M.*

**See also pages 108, 109, 174**

Jacob with Laban and his Daughters, 1676
*London, Dulwich Coll. Gall.*

28

By the end of the 1630's Claude had established a reputation as a landscape painter. He was the first to realize the picturesque possibilities of the Campagna, the countryside around Rome, and he wandered over it sketching in pen, in wash and perhaps even in oils. In these fresh and vivid sketches he caught the intrinsic light effects of the Campagna, and in his finished canvases he used the pervading quality of the light to bind his subjects together. He often set his rustic scenes in a landscape with a dark brown foreground, light brown and green for the old buildings and trees of the middle distance, and a background that stretches away into pale blue infinity. Especially in his later works, the human figure is reduced to insignificance, and the paintings are lyrical and imaginative in feeling. Claude was almost illiterate, but he never lacked patrons. He died in 1682, a respected member of the Roman colony of artists.

A. M. Hind   The Drawings of Claude Lorraine   New York, 1925
M. Röthlisberger   Claude   New Haven, Conn., 1961

Seaport: The Embarkation
of St. Ursula, 1641
*London, N. G.*

Italian Landscape, 1658
*London, Wallace Coll.*

Landscape with Tobias and the Angel
*London, N. G.*

Landscape: The Marriage of Isaac
and Rebekah (The Mill) (detail) 1648
*London, N. G.*

Montesquieu, begun 1779
*Paris, Institut de France*

## HIS WORKS INCLUDE

The Arts (terracotta reliefs)
*Cherbourg, Mus.*

Vase (marble) 1782
*London, Wallace Coll.*

The Triumph of Galatea (relief)
*Paris, Mus. Jacquemart-André*

Erigone
*Maisons-Lafitte, Château*

**See also page 209**

*A Rococo sculptor*

Clodion, whose real name was Claude Michel, was born in Nancy, in 1738. Both his parents came from families of sculptors, and his first master was his uncle, Lambert Sigisbert Adam. Later he studied under Jean Baptiste Pigalle, and the sculptor Augustin Pajou was his father-in-law. Between 1762 and 1771 Clodion was in Rome.

On his return to Paris, Clodion began to build a reputation as "the Fragonard of terracotta," because his subjects—nymphs, fauns, bacchantes, and putti — resembled those of Jean Honoré Fragonard. There were, as well, a few more ambitious state commissions. Clodion began a marble *St. Cecilia* in 1774 for Rouen Cathedral, and, later, a *Crucified Christ* for the same cathedral. In 1779 he received a royal commission for a statue of Montesquieu, for the Institut de France. The lively pose and expression of the work show Clodion's acute perception of the character of this dynamic man.

The Revolution of 1789 ruined Clodion as it ruined Fragonard and all the fashionable favorites of the last years of the monarchy. Clodion, however, managed to adopt the prevalent Neoclassicism with some success, and from 1806 worked on the Colonne de la Grande Armée and the Arc de Triomphe du Carrousel. These do little more than reflect the taste of the time, and Clodion's fame rests on his more exuberant and unforced early works. All his subjects owe a great deal to his studies in Rome. Clodion died in 1814.

Bacchante and Satyr
*Paris, Louvre*

Satyr with a Tambourine
*Paris, Louvre*

# FRANÇOIS CLOUET

died 1572

*A celebrated portrait painter*

François Clouet was born in Tours some time before 1520. He was the son of Jean Clouet the Younger, and he succeeded his father as Painter to the King in 1540, so it is probable that he was already celebrated by this date. The style of François Clouet's work suggests that he might have visited Italy at some time. His portraits conform to a type common to International Mannerism, but the most important influence on his work was that of the Flemish painters.

Only two signed paintings by Clouet have survived. The first is his earliest known work, the portrait of his friend, the apothecary Pierre Quthe, painted in 1562. The greatest number of Clouet's existing works are drawings of court notabilities but he also carried out decorations, supervised the court artists, and painted mythological scenes. In the latter part of the 16th century portrait painters continued to work in the way that Clouet had evolved. Some influence from his father's work is apparent, but François Clouet put greater emphasis on texture and detail.

The second signed painting is the *Lady at Her Toilet*, which is one of the first examples of a theme that was to become popular with the 16th-century painters. The painting is among the most original creations of the School of Fontainebleau, and is traditionally supposed to represent Diane de Poitiers. In fact, it is probably a portrait of Marie Touchet. A pronounced Flemish influence is evident in the treatment of the figure and the still-life elements in the picture. Another picture, the *Bath of Diana*, exists in several versions, one of which depicts the royal mistress Gabrielle d'Estrées; it is more Italianate in design. François Clouet died in Paris in 1572.

ANONYMOUS
Portrait of François Clouet
*Paris, Bibl. Nat.*

HIS WORKS INCLUDE

Series of Portraits (drawings)
*Chantilly, Mus. Condé*
Lady at her Toilet
*Washington, D.C., N.G., Kress Coll.*

**See also pages 95, 166**

Charles IX of France, 1570
*Vienna, Kunsthist. Mus.*

Francis I
*Florence, Uffizi*

Elizabeth of Austria
*Paris, Louvre*

31

## JEAN CLOUET

died 1540/1

*A portrait artist who worked primarily in black or red chalk*

Francis I
*Paris, Louvre*

Jean Clouet is believed to have been the son of a painter who worked for the Duke of Burgundy. The date of his birth is unknown, but the place was almost certainly somewhere in the Netherlands. Jean Clouet is mentioned in a poem of 1509 by Lemaire de Belges, and from 1516 his name occurs in the royal accounts. The accounts show that at first the payments to Jean Clouet were less than those to Jean Perréal and Jean Bourdichon, but on the disappearance of Bourdichon's name from the accounts in 1521 Jean Clouet became Perréal's equal in wages.

Not many paintings can be attributed to Jean Clouet with any certainty, as even those that are obviously after his drawings may have been painted by another hand. His method of shading his drawings may have been learned from the work of Leonardo, who was in France from 1517 until his death in 1519. At any rate, it shows that Jean Clouet's style was not entirely derived from the north. Jean Clouet was appointed Painter to the King by Francis I, and on his death his son François followed him in this post.

HIS WORKS INCLUDE

The Dauphin François, about 1525
*Antwerp, Mus. Royal des B-A.*
Guillaume Budé, about 1534
*New York, Met. Mus.*

**See also page 164**

---

## MICHEL COLOMBE

about 1430/35 - after 1512

*A celebrated sculptor of the early Renaissance in France*

Relief from the Altarpiece of St. George, from the Chapel at Gaillon, 1508-9
*Paris, Louvre*

Michel Colombe was born probably some time between 1430 and 1435. There is almost no information about his production until early in the 16th century, when he is recorded as working on two important pieces of sculpture. The first was the tomb of the Duke of Brittany, Francis II, in Nantes Cathedral. In 1500 Anne of Brittany had collected marble for the tomb and commissioned Girolamo da Fiesole, an Italian sculptor, to carry out the work, but by the end of the same year she had approached Colombe and Jean Perréal. Two years later they began, and the tomb was completed in 1507. It appears that Perréal designed the tomb, and Colombe worked out the detail of the sculpture.

In the relief from the *Altarpiece of St. George*, which Colombe executed between 1508 and 1509 for the Chapel at Gaillon, there are stronger traces of Italian influence, but the feeling is still predominantly northern. His work represents a most important element in the transition between Gothic and Renaissance style in France. A celebrated sculptor in his own day, he is last recorded in 1512.

HIS WORKS INCLUDE

Louis XII (gold medal) 1500
*Paris, Louvre*

**See also page 195**

# JEAN BAPTISTE CAMILLE COROT 1796-1875

*A painter of misty landscapes*

Corot was born in Paris on July 16, 1796, the son of a cloth merchant and a milliner. When he left school he worked with a firm of textile dealers for a short time to please his father, but from 1822 his father gave him an annual stipend and he was able to devote himself to painting. He studied first with Achille Michallon and then with Jean Victor Bertin, both landscape painters in the classical tradition.

In 1825 Corot made his first journey to Italy, remaining there until the autumn of 1828. He visited Rome, Naples, and Venice, and he painted landscapes of the Roman countryside, two of which were exhibited in the Salon of 1827.

Corot gained a second class medal in 1833 for a landscape painted in the Fontainebleau Forest. He returned to Italy in 1834, traveling via Lyons and Marseilles to Genoa. After some weeks he went to Tuscany, to Venice, and to the neighboring lakes. The following years Corot spent most of his time at Fontainebleau, making landscape studies. He became a regular exhibitor at the Salon, though the paintings he showed were composed from sketches, and often lacked the freshness and lost some of the exact quality of light that Corot considered important. In 1840 he painted a *Flight into Egypt*, which he exhibited with *The Little Shepherd*, at the Salon. Two years later he made the first of many subsequent journeys to Switzerland.

It was in 1843 that Corot visited Italy for the third time; he stayed in the vicinity of Rome, where he made numerous drawings and small freely handled sketches.

Self-portrait
*Florence, Uffizi*

A Leaning Tree by the Water's Edge
*Reims, Mus. des B-A.*

Woman with a Pearl, about 1868-70
*Paris, Louvre*

33

The Belfry at Douai, 1871
*Paris, Louvre*

HIS WORKS INCLUDE

View of Florence, about 1835
*Paris, Louvre*

St. André-en-Morvan, 1842
*Paris, Louvre*

A Seated Monk Reading, 1850-55
*Paris, Louvre*

A Leaning Tree Trunk, 1855-60
*London, N. G.*

Velléda, about 1870
*Paris, Louvre*

**See also pages 150, 151, 152, 190**

Several years later he was given a commission for *The Baptism of Christ*, in the Church of St. Nicolas-du-Chardonnet in Paris. By this time his reputation was well established, and he was awarded the Legion of Honor in 1846. Corot became a member of the Salon jury in 1848, and did all he could to help painters who refused to conform to academic requirements. His prestige with the younger generation was very great.

Corot traveled widely in France, first between 1827 and 1831, and then in the early 1850's. In 1855 he exhibited six paintings in the Universal Exhibition and was awarded a first class medal. The Emperor bought one of his paintings, and his work was at once in great demand. In his later years Corot produced a series of religious paintings and began to concentrate on figure compositions and portraits. He spent a week in London in 1862 and in the same year made the acquaintance of Gustave Courbet at Saintonge. He exhibited seven canvases in the 1867 Universal Exhibition and was awarded a second class medal and was made an Officer of the Legion of Honor. After a long and successful career Corot died in 1875. He was a kindly man who helped Daumier in his last years and supported Millet's widow when she was left penniless.

Chartres Cathedral, 1830
*Paris, Louvre*

The Road to Arras, about 1872
*Paris, Louvre*

# GUSTAVE COURBET

*The founder of Realism*

Gustave Courbet was born at Ornans on June 10, 1819, of prosperous peasant stock. His grandfather had strong republican tendencies, which had their influence on the young Courbet. His character was singularly aggressive and his art was closely related to it. He disliked study and was violently anti-clerical, interested only in painting and drawing. In Besançon he studied with a disciple of Jacques Louis David, who taught him to fill his sketch-books with portraits and details of street scenes.

In 1840 Courbet went to Paris. He was not interested in academic institutions and instead attended the Atelier Suisse where for a small fee the students could draw or paint the model however they wished. This atelier was important for 19th-century French painting: Delacroix worked there twenty years earlier, Paul Cézanne and Camille Pissarro twenty years later.

Courbet spent several years painting in Paris and Ornans. He exhibited in the Salons of 1844 and 1845 and regularly from then on. In 1847 he visited Holland, admiring the Dutch painters, particularly Rembrandt. He was strongly influenced by the naturalistic painting of the 17th-century Dutch school.

1848 was a year of revolution in Europe, and in France King Louis Philippe was

NADAR
Gustave Courbet (photo)

The Stone Breakers, about 1850
*Winterthur, Switzerland, coll. Oscar Reinhart*

Hector Berlioz, 1850
*Paris, Louvre*

The Pool
*London, N. G.*

HIS WORKS INCLUDE

Self-portrait, 1847
*Montpellier, Mus. Fabre*

Man with a Leather Belt, 1848
*Paris, Louvre*

After Dinner at Ornans, 1849
*Lille, Pal. des B-A.*

"Bonjours Monsieur Courbet," 1854
*Montpellier, Mus. Fabre*

The Painter's Studio, 1855
*Paris, Louvre*

Young Ladies by the Seine,
1856
*Paris, Petit-Palais*

The Diligence in the Snow, 1860
*London, N. G.*

**See also page 160**

forced to abdicate. Courbet was horrified at the repression and the slaughter that followed, and spurred on by his new friendship with the socialist Proud'hon, he assumed the part of politician and social philosopher.

His art could not be untouched by his socialistic convictions. Between 1848 and 1850 he painted four of his largest and most important works, *After Dinner at Ornans*, *The Stone Breakers*, *Burial at Ornans*, and *Return from the Fair*. It was then usual for genre paintings to be small, and Courbet shattered all precedent by making the figures almost life-size.

One canvas sums up Courbet's somewhat confused theories of Realism. This was *The Painter's Studio*, an intended allegory of contemporary life. When the authorities refused to exhibit this work at the 1855 Paris exhibition, Courbet organized his own private exhibition and called it the Pavilion of Realism.

Meanwhile Courbet was painting landscapes out of doors and finishing them indoors, figures being added in the studio. Two works of this kind, the large *Bathers* and the *Wrestlers*, caused a scandal at the 1853 Salon and Eugène Delacroix described them as vulgar.

In the mid-1860's Courbet became fashionable. His range of subjects was wide and varied. Landscapes, portraits, still-lifes, animals in the snow, and hunting scenes were all treated with vitality and directness.

The last years of Courbet's life were disturbed ones. During the Commune of 1871 he was named President of a Committee formed to preserve works of art. As a consequence of this appointment, he became involved in the demolition of the Vendôme column, a monument to detested Imperial glory. When the Commune collapsed, Courbet was tried and imprisoned. In 1873 the Assembly decided to make him pay for reconstruction of the column. He fled to Switzerland, where he died in 1877.

G. Mack  *Gustave Courbet*  London, 1952
M. Zahar  *Gustave Courbet*  London, 1951

In the Forest
*London, N. G.*

Still-life: Apples and Pomegranates, 1871
*London, N. G.*

# ANTOINE COYSEVOX

*A master of a vigorous Baroque style*

Antoine Coysevox was born in Lyons in 1640. From 1657 he studied at the school of the Academy in Paris, and he worked under the sculptor Louis Lerambert for six years. He never went to Italy, and Classicism did not come naturally to him.

Coysevox's earliest work is a *Madonna* which shows that he had learned much from Jacques Sarrazin. By 1679 he was working at Versailles. There he was often required to copy classical models, under the close supervision of Charles Lebrun and Louis XIV's minister Colbert. These works are not, on the whole, very successful, although they pleased the taste of the time. In the decoration of the later rooms of the palace—the Hall of Mirrors, l'Escalier des Ambassadeurs, and the Salon de la Guerre—Coysevox worked more happily and effectively.

In the Salon de la Guerre Coysevox's noblest piece of real sculpture, as against decoration, is to be found. This is the relief of Louis XIV, mounted and victorious, set into an oval frame on the wall. The work is designed at a diagonal to the plane of the wall, so that the horse appears to be about to leap free of the relief. In this work Coysevox has given free rein to his Baroque inclinations. The tendency persisted and was intensified in later sculptures. In 1689 he began the tomb of Cardinal Mazarin, in which the gesture and draperies are Baroque, though classical elements still occur. This was finished in 1693.

The taste of the 1690's, following the death of Colbert and Lebrun, softened toward the Baroque. The classical sculptor François Giraudon lost his popularity, while his rival Coysevox gained it. Coysevox's kneeling statue of Louis XIV is strongly Baroque, while *The Duchess of Burgundy as Diana* with its fluttering draperies and light tread, verges on the Rococo. In 1689 he made a bronze statue of Louis XIV, now in the Musée Carnavalet.

It is in the portrait busts of his last years that Coysevox attained real originality. When portraying his friends, he dropped the formality of his court style, and concentrated on penetrating and revealing character. In the alert twist of the head of *Robert de Cotte*, 1707, with its untidy hair and minimum of drapery, there is a naturalism new to French sculpture.

Coysevox had begun to form the idea of Rococo sculpture, and Antoine Watteau had drawn such sculpture in the backgrounds of his paintings before Coysevox's death in 1720, but it was not to be the prevalent manner in France until the late 1730's. After his death Coysevox's two nephews, the brothers Guillaume and Nicolas Coustou, continued to work in his tradition.

The Glory of Louis XIV, about 1680
*Versailles, Château*

## HIS WORKS INCLUDE

Madonna, 1676
*Lyons, St. Nizier*

Portrait of Charles Lebrun, 1676
*London, Wallace Coll.*

Monument to Colbert, about 1687
*Paris, St. Eustache*

Reliefs (bronze) for the equestrian statue of Louis XIV, 1692
*Rennes, Mus. de Rennes*

Portrait Bust of Matthew Prior, 1700
*London, Westminster Abbey*

Portrait of Robert de Cotte, 1707
*Paris, Bibl. Nat.*

**See also page 203**

The Tomb of Cardinal Mazarin
1689-93
*Paris, Institut de France*

Self-portrait
*Avignon, Mus. Calvet*

h. Daumier

## HONORÉ DAUMIER

*A brilliant caricaturist*

Honoré Daumier was born in Marseilles on February 26, 1808. His father was a glazier and frame-maker. In 1816 the family moved to Paris, where Daumier was to spend most of his life. He worked as an office boy, then as a clerk with a bookseller in the Palais Royal. His only interest, however, was drawing, and in 1822 he was allowed to study at the Académie Suisse.

In 1825 Honoré Daumier entered the workshop of the printer Zéphirin-Félix Belliard and worked as a studio assistant, gaining a training in lithography. He began to produce, at this time, brilliant cartoons for the socialist papers, but Daumier soon found himself in trouble. In 1831 he caricatured King Louis Philippe as Rabelais' Gargantua and was fined and imprisoned. He was released in February, 1833. In August, 1835, the government muzzled the press for which Daumier worked. *Le Charivari*, another publication to which he contributed, was forced to abandon political satire, and be content with ridicule of the bourgeois society.

From 1835 to 1845 Daumier published a vast number of lithographs, creating at this time the figure of "Robert Macaire," in whose person society was violently lampooned.

### HIS WORKS INCLUDE

The Republic (sketch) 1848
*Paris, Louvre*

Refugees, about 1855
*Paris, Petit-Palais*

The Barrel Organ (watercolor)
about 1860
*Paris, Petit-Palais*

The Collector, about 1860
*Paris, Petit-Palais*

Scene from Molière, about 1860
*Paris, Louvre*

The Washerwoman, 1861
*Paris, Louvre*

The Chess Players, about 1863
*Paris, Petit-Palais*

**See also pages 156, 191**

The Third Class Carriage
*New York, Met. Mus.*

Crispin and Scapin
*Paris, Louvre*

In 1848 came the fall of Louis Philippe, and during the short-lived Second Republic artistic affairs were suddenly in the hands of the more liberal-minded artist. Everything submitted to the Salon was hung. By December, 1848, the Republic was finished, and Louis Napoleon had been proclaimed emperor. Radical tendencies were again subdued.

In 1849 Daumier was commissioned by the State to paint a religious picture; eventually however the Ministry accepted *The Drunkenness of Silenus* instead. In this year he also exhibited *The Miller, His Son, and the Ass* at the Salon. This picture, and similarly *Nymphs Pursued by Satyrs* exhibited the following year, were not appreciated by the critics. His spontaneous, sketchy style was far in advance of his own time and was understood only by a few fellow painters. Millet's painting, for instance, was influenced by Daumier in both style and subject matter.

Honoré Daumier executed a few works of sculpture. One of the most expressive is the figure of Ratapoil, who embodied all the ignominy and vice of contemporary society. He also treated the subject of refugees in a bas-relief of about 1851. His

Grand Stairway in the Palais de Justice,
*Baltimore, Md., Mus. of Art*

Don Quixote and Sancho Panza Going to the Wedding of Camacho, 1851
*London, Tate*

39

attempt to branch out as a painter was unsuccessful. He worked in both water-color and oil, turning to everyday life for his subject matter.

In 1868 Daumier left Paris for Valmondois, where Corot gave him a house. He was still harnessed to the never-ending production of lithographs in order to make a living. His later paintings, mainly of the Don Quixote theme, were unique in their freedom of handling. In 1873 he began to go blind, and in February, 1879, he died.

J. Lassaigne  Daumier  London, 1957
K. E. Maison  Daumier Drawings  London, 1960

Nymphs Pursued by Satyrs
*Montreal, Mus. of Fine Arts*

Self-portrait, 1794
*Paris, Louvre*

## HIS WORKS INCLUDE

Combat of Minerva and Mars, 1771
*Paris, Louvre*

The Death of Socrates, 1787
*New York, Met. Mus.*

Brutus with his Dead Son, 1789
*Paris, Louvre*

The Sabines, 1799
*Paris, Louvre*

The Presentation of the Eagles, 1810
*Versailles, Mus.*

Léonidas in Thermopiles, 1814
*Paris, Louvre*

**See also pages 137, 138, 139**

# JACQUES LOUIS DAVID

1748-1825

*The first and most successful of the Neoclassical painters*

The son of a Paris haberdasher, Jacques Louis David, a distant relation of Boucher, was born in Paris in 1748. In 1766 he entered Joseph Vien's studio, and in the same year became a student at the Academy. Although he was influenced by the growing antique revival in French art, his earliest work shows the impact of his relation, Boucher, rather than that of his master. He won the Prix de Rome in 1774 after failing several times, and in 1775 he went to Rome with Vien. There he met the antiquarian Quatremère de Quincy and the sculptor Jean Baptiste Giraud, who awoke in him an enthusiasm for ancient sculpture that with the painting of Poussin was to form the basis of his Neoclassic style.

This enthusiasm for the classical ideal began to show in David's work with his *Belisarius*, which was exhibited at the 1781 Salon. Two years later he returned to Rome to continue work on his next picture, *The Oath of the Horatii*. All Rome flocked to his studio to see it, and all Paris to the Salon when it was shown there in 1785. *The Oath of the Horatii* became the prototype for all such grand and monumental works, inspiring those who were to lead the Revolution of 1789 with the ideal of patriotic duty it expresses.

David himself became one of those leaders. A member of the Third Estate, he loathed the monarchy and all it stood for, and he loathed the Academy. He was a fervent supporter of Robespierre, and voted for the death of Louis XVI. His cruelly indifferent sketch of Marie-Antoinette on her way to the guillotine is in sharp contrast to his painting of *The Death of Marat* (who was stabbed by Charlotte Corday while in his bath), in which he invests the revolutionary leader with the simple dignity of a martyred saint.

40

On August 8, 1793, David brought about the dissolution of the Academy. He created a new system for the control of the arts, the Commune of the Arts, which had 300 members. His own painting continued to reflect the exalted republican feelings evident in his *The Death of Socrates* and *Brutus with His Dead Son*, which had been exhibited in 1789 during the assembly of the Estates General and the assault on the Bastille. In fact, though the scenes chosen by David were revolutionary, his style was rational and ordered in the extreme. This is strongly apparent if his paintings are compared with, for instance, Delacroix's *Liberty Guiding the People* of 1830.

David lost his revolutionary fervor after his imprisonment in the Luxembourg Palace following the fall of Robespierre, but in 1798 he met Napoleon and became an ardent Bonapartist. During the 1790's he painted some portraits, which are among his best works, though he thought them trivial. Napoleon honored David, realizing his value as a superb tool of propaganda. He commissioned him to paint a huge scene of the Imperial coronation in 1805, and many other pictures celebrating Napoleonic glory. For 20 years David was the unchallenged head of the official school in France. As the greatest teacher of the time, he attracted many promising young painters to his studio. Among his pupils were Ingres, Gros, and the successful portrait painter, François Gérard.

After the battle of Waterloo in 1815, which was followed by the restoration of the Bourbon monarchy, David fled to Brussels where he spent the last years of his life. He died in 1825.

*D. L. Dowd   J. L. David and the French Revolution   Lincoln, Nebraska, 1948*

Pope Pius VII, 1805
*Paris, Louvre*

*L. David*

The Coronation of Napoleon and Josephine in Notre Dame, about 1807
*Paris, Louvre*

Portrait of Monsieur Sériziat, 1795
*Paris, Louvre*

Self-portrait
*Florence, Uffizi*

**EUG. DELACROIX**

*The leader of the Romantic school of painters*

Eugène Delacroix was born at Saint-Maurice just outside Paris in 1798. His mother was the wife of a distinguished civil servant, Charles Delacroix, and he was probably the son of the diplomat Talleyrand. Showing his talent early, he entered the studio of the undistinguished but tolerant painter Baron Guérin. There he met Géricault, for whom he had great respect. He admired Antoine Jean Gros, and studied the works of Michelangelo and Rubens, from whom he learned the use of color.

Delacroix made his Salon debut in 1822 with a picture of *Dante and Virgil Crossing the Styx*, an unusual subject chosen for its power to horrify the spectator. He went further at the 1824 Salon by depicting a contemporary event of notorious brutality, *The Massacre at Chios*. In style, the picture shows the influence of Gros and of John Constable, whose *Hay-Wain* was shown at the same Salon. Delacroix had for some time been very interested in English art and literature, especially Shakespeare, Scott, and Byron. He was very friendly with the watercolorist Richard Parkes Bonington, with whom he spent the summer of 1825 in England.

The Greek War of Independence, in which by 1830 the Greeks had won their freedom from the Turkish Empire, captured Delacroix's imagination as it had Byron's. In fact, the theme of his painting *The Death of Sardanapalus*, shown at the Salon of 1829, was taken from a poem by Byron. It caused a scandal on account of its brilliant color and violent, exotic subject. The Vicomte Sosthène de la Rochefoucauld told Delacroix that he must change his style if he hoped for state commissions. Delacroix, although he could well have done with the financial security of official patronage, replied that he would go on in his own way "though the earth and the stars were on the other side."

Dante and Virgil Crossing the Styx, 1822
*Paris, Louvre*

The Death of Sardanapalus, 1827
*Paris, Louvre*

The Revolution of 1830 brought Louis Philippe to the throne of France. Inspired by the Revolution, Delacroix painted his allegorical picture of *Liberty Guiding the People*, which was exhibited in 1831. In 1832 he accompanied a diplomatic mission to the Sultan of Morocco. Although unable to paint much, he made many drawings and sketches. Delacroix was the first great artist to visit the Islamic countries of North Africa, and the colorful and exotic nature of the places and people he saw was exactly suited to stimulate his genius. On his return he painted many North African scenes, such as the equestrian portrait of the Sultan of Morocco, the *Women of Algiers*, and *The Jewish Wedding*.

From 1832 Delacroix began to receive official commissions through his friend Louis Adolphe Thiers, who had become a minister in that year. Between 1838 and 1854 he executed large-scale decorative schemes for the Salon du Roi and Library of the Senate, the Gallery of Apollo in the Louvre, and the Town Hall of Paris. His last and most influential wall paintings are *Jacob and the Angel* and *Heliodorus* (1857-61), in a chapel of the Church of St. Sulpice. All the time he was painting many easel pictures of subjects from classical and medieval history, Shakespeare, Oriental legend, as well as portraits of his intimate friends, Chopin among them,

Baron Schwiter, 1830
*London, N. G.*

Hamlet and Horatio in the Graveyard, 1859
*Paris, Louvre*

Abel Widmer, about 1824
*London, N. G.*

and studies of fighting animals. Delacroix's energy did not fail him with increasing years; the International Exhibition of 1855 was a personal triumph.

In spite of his success, Delacroix was not a happy man. He wrote, "Almost all great men lead a life more thwarted, more miserable than that of other men." This melancholy is to be expected of the leader of the Romantic School in French painting, and yet he also wrote, in direct contradiction of Romantic theories, "The greatest genius is but a more highly rational being." His letters and his diary, kept between 1822 and 1824 and again from 1847 until his death, give a most valuable picture of his life and character. He had no pupils and no artistic successors, in spite of the affectionate respect he won from younger artists. He died in Paris in 1863.

*Delacroix (trans. L. Norton)  Journal  London, 1951*
*Charles Baudelaire  The Mirror of Art  London, 1955*

Ovid Among the Scythians, 1859
*London, N. G.*

---

ÉTIENNE DELAUNE                                          about 1518-1583

*An engraver of great technical excellence*

Étienne Delaune was born in Orléans, and became a metalworker, engraver, and draftsman, but little is known of his life. He worked as an engraver of medals, and was employed in the Mint. During his career in France he made numerous copperplate reproductions of various works of the School of Fontainebleau, and his drawings show the distinct influence of Mannerism. Delaune is known to have worked with Benvenuto Cellini during Cellini's stay in France, and to some extent his technique of engraving was influenced by him. He produced several sets of original work, including the *Twelve Months of the Year*, and illustrations to the Old Testament. Because he belonged to the Protestant faith, Delaune was forced to take refuge in Strasbourg when Charles IX began his persecution, and he remained there for the rest of his life.

## TOUSSAINT DUBREUIL                                    1561-1602

*A forerunner of French Classicism*

Toussaint Dubreuil was born in Paris, and became an artist of the Second School of Fontainebleau. It is possible that he was trained by the painter Médéric Fréminet, and he was certainly greatly influenced by the work of the Italians Primaticcio and Niccolò dell'Abbate. He was appointed Painter in Ordinary to Henry III, and then to Henry IV, and his work included the planning of many decorations in the Tuileries, Fontainebleau, Saint-Germain-en-Laye, and the Louvre. Almost all the works carried out by Dubreuil have since been destroyed or have disappeared without trace. He is known to have executed a series of paintings in the Petite Galerie of the Louvre (now the Gallery of Apollo), but these were lost in the fire of 1661.

His few remaining works include the *Antique Sacrifice*, and two sets of tapestries, made at Gobelins after his cartoons, representing the histories of Psyche and Diana. They indicate, as do his drawings, the extent to which he was influenced by the Italian Mannerist painters. His work shows greater restraint than that of most of his contemporaries. His feeling for clarity and equilibrium make him a forerunner of Classicism, and a link between the Mannerists and the ideas of Poussin in the next century.

Antique Sacrifice
*Paris, Louvre*

**See also page 167**

---

## GASPARD DUGHET or GASPARD POUSSIN                    1615-1675

*A pupil and imitator of Nicolas Poussin*

Gaspard Dughet, or Poussin, adopted the name of his famous master and brother-in-law, Nicolas Poussin. A landscape painter, he spent most of his life working in Rome and its vicinity. For more than three years he studied with Nicolas Poussin, probably from 1630, and he knew the Italian Salvator Rosa. His work reflects not only the teaching of Poussin, but also the influence of Claude Lorraine. His earlier work is in a more romantic style, and owes something to the paintings of Adam Elsheimer and Paul Bril, with Mannerist compositions and strong contrasts of light. He was celebrated among his contemporaries for his precocity and the rapidity with which he painted.

At some time in the late 1640's Dughet painted frescoes in the Church of San Martino al Monte and the Palazzo Doria Pamphili in Rome. His mature work represents a balance between the styles of Claude and of Poussin, and has some of Claude's lyricism and feeling for light. He was greatly admired by English painters, such as Richard Wilson, and his paintings were used as models for landscape gardens and parks.

The Falls of Tivoli
*London, Wallace Coll.*

**HIS WORKS INCLUDE**

Ariccia
*London, N. G.*
Frescoes, 1645-50
*Rome, S. Martino al Monte*
Landscapes
*Rome, Pal. Colonna*

**See also page 175**

## PIERRE DUMONSTIER II
about 1565-1656

*A meticulous draftsman*

Pierre Dumonstier II was born in Paris in about 1565. His father was Étienne Dumonstier, one of three brothers all of whom were court artists to Catherine de' Medici.

Few facts are known about Pierre. However, it is generally believed that he spent most of his life in Rome, returning to Paris permanently only in old age. He worked mainly in three-color crayon and chalk. His drawings, though meticulous in technique, carry on a tradition in portraiture founded by Jean and François Clouet.

Portrait of Madame Lenoir (detail)
about 1769  *Paris, Louvre*

## JOSEPH SIFFREIN DUPLESSIS
1725-1802

*A portrait painter*

Born at Carpentras in 1725, Joseph Siffrein Duplessis was the son of a famous surgeon who gave up his profession to become a painter.

In 1745 Duplessis went to Rome and remained there until 1749. In Paris from 1752, he quickly made a name as a portrait painter, and was elected to the Academy in 1774. Soon afterwards he was appointed painter to the king. Noble families, painters, sculptors, and prelates of the church made up the clientele for his penetrating, personal portraits, which include paintings of famous men such as the composer Gluck, the financier Necker, and Benjamin Franklin. They show the model in the unguarded moments of his private life, with no trace of the Grand Manner.

On the outbreak of the Revolution, Duplessis defended the Academy but was reduced to poverty and retired to Carpentras in 1792. Returning to Paris in 1796, he was appointed Keeper of the Museum of Versailles. He died in 1802.

Milo of Crotona
*Paris, Louvre*

## ÉTIENNE MAURICE FALCONET
1716-1791

*A sculptor who excelled in graceful allegorical works*

Falconet was born in Paris in 1716, where he grew up in humble circumstances. He became the pupil first of Nicolas Guillaume and then of Jean Baptiste Lemoyne, in whose studio he produced the *Milo of Crotona*, which enabled him to become an Associate of the Academy. Ten years later he was made an Academician, and in 1761 he became a professor. *La Baigneuse*, one of the best known of his works, was exhibited in the Salon of 1757. In 1758 Falconet was appointed director of sculpture at the Sèvres Manufactory, and many models of his work were produced in biscuit ware. He remained in this post for some years, but eventually became dissatisfied with the opportunities it offered him. The Russian Empress, Catherine II, was determined to infuse her court with French culture, and she welcomed French artists. In 1766 Falconet was given permission to go to Russia, and during his stay he designed and executed a large bronze statue of Peter the Great. He remained there until 1781.

Falconet became one of the most notable figures in the art world of his day. In 1761 he published his "Reflections on Sculpture," in which he rigorously criticized the slavish followers of the classical canons. He was most celebrated for his sculptures of nymphs and goddesses, in which the warmth and softness of the human body was sensitively expressed. His serious works include powerful and originally treated sacred subjects.

HIS WORKS INCLUDE

Music, 1751
*Paris, Louvre*
La Baigneuse, 1757
*Paris, Louvre*
Cupid, 1757
*Paris, Louvre*
Bust of Arztes Camille Falconet, 1761
*Angers, Mus. des B-A.*

**See also page 208**

---

# JEAN FOUQUET  about 1420 - about 1481

*A painter whose work represents the high point of art in 15th-century France*

Jean Fouquet was born at Tours about 1420, and was probably the illegitimate son of a priest. There is documentary evidence to prove that he had been to Rome before 1447, for he is mentioned by Filarete, the Florentine architect and sculptor, as having painted there a portrait of Pope Eugenius IV with two of his nephews. This pope died in 1447. Another proof of Fouquet's Italian journey is to be found in his miniatures, several of which accurately depict Roman monuments.

On his return to Tours, probably about 1447, Fouquet was employed by the king, Charles VII, and by great men of his court. He must have set up a studio in Tours, and he carried out decorations in the Church of Notre-Dame-La-Riche. Fouquet may well have been trained in Paris; views of the city appear in the *Book of Hours of Étienne Chevalier*, which may date from between 1450 and 1455. This series of illuminations displays also a knowledge of Italian art, particularly of the works of Fra Angelico, whose frescoes in the Vatican Fouquet may well have seen. The illustrations for the *Book of Hours* represent the highest point of his art, and indicate the monumental, classical style that is typical of all his work. For Étienne Chevalier he also painted the *Melun Diptych*, which is probably his best-known work. In the panel representing the Madonna with Angels, the figure of the Madonna is said to be a portrait of Agnès Sorel, the king's mistress. The portrait of Chevalier as donor is an outstanding example of Fouquet's ability as a portraitist. A work that may have been painted before Fouquet's visit to Rome is his portrait of Charles VII, though the inscription "Charles VII... most victorious King of France" would seem to place the picture in the early 1450's.

Fouquet executed many miniatures. These include illustrations to Josephus' *Jewish Antiquities*, the *Chronicles of the Kings of France* and tales by Boccaccio, as well as the *Hours of Étienne Chevalier*. In his last works there is evidence of a change in style, away from the monumental and toward a more decorative, crowded type of composition. In 1472 he was summoned to Blois to illuminate a prayer book for Marie of Cleves, the widow of Charles of Orléans, and four years later he worked

Self-portrait
*Paris, Louvre*

The Virgin Mother Receiving the Homage of Étienne Chevalier (detail) about 1450-55
*Chantilly, Mus. Condé*

for Cardinal Charles of Bourbon. Fouquet was appointed Painter to the King in 1475. When Louis XI succeeded his father in 1461 he continued to extend the royal patronage to the painter. Fouquet's influence on French painting was far reaching, equivalent to that of the van Eycks in Flanders, and Masaccio in Italy.

He died in Tours before November 8, 1481; a record of that date in his parish church refers to his widow and heirs.

*C. Winkworth   Jean Fouquet and His Time   London, 1947*

Self-portrait
*Paris, Private Collection*

# JEAN HONORÉ FRAGONARD 1732-1806

*The most typical and successful painter of courtly subjects in the second half of the 18th century*

Jean Honoré Fragonard was born in Provence in 1732, and went to Paris as a young man. For a short time in 1750 he was a pupil of Chardin, but he soon went to Boucher, who was then at the height of his prestige and talent. Fragonard was influenced by Boucher's subject matter, and by his rich yet delicate color and spontaneous line. In 1752 Fragonard won the Prix de Rome, though he spent several years in Paris, under Carle van Loo, specializing in history painting, before he traveled to Italy in 1756, accompanied by Hubert Robert. Together they visited many parts of the country, going as far south as Sicily. During this period Fragonard made many drawings of gardens and monuments. He worked at the French Academy in Rome until 1761.

Boucher fell ill soon after Fragonard's return to Paris in 1761, and Fragonard produced a number of paintings for his master's patrons. Following the success of his painting of *The High Priest Coresus Sacrificing himself to Save Callirrhoë*, 1765, he was made an Associate of the Academy. After a short time Fragonard turned to a lighter type of subject, and depicted *fêtes galantes*, mythological scenes, and episodes of court life, often with an erotic undertone. He received many commissions from the court circles, and from 1770 worked mainly as a decorative painter. Among his decorations is a series of paintings entitled *The Progress of Love*, for Madame du Barry's house in Louveciennes, which was inexplicably rejected.

The Cradle
*Amiens, Mus. de Picardie*

The Bathers
*Paris, Louvre*

The Music Lesson
*Paris, Louvre*

About 1772 Fragonard made a journey to the Netherlands; he greatly admired both Rembrandt and Rubens, and Rembrandt's paintings, many of which he copied, were to have an important influence on his work. He was particularly interested in Rembrandt's deep shadows and sudden shafts of light. In 1772 he returned to Italy, where he made many drawings, particularly in Rome, Tivoli, and the neighboring countryside. Fragonard's career came to an end with the French Revolution, and in 1789 he fled to Grasse to avoid the terror. His poverty forced him to return to Paris, but there was no longer any demand for his type of work. The painter David found him a job in the Museums Service, and he died in obscurity in 1806.

G. Wildenstein  The Paintings of Fragonard  New York, London, 1960
E. and G. Seligman  Portraits by Fragonard, Paintings and Drawings  New York, 1961

## NICOLAS FROMENT                                                   active 1450-1490

*A 15th-century court artist*

Nicolas Froment, a 15th-century painter born in Uzès, was active in the south of France. He was court painter to René I, Duke of Anjou and Lorraine and King of Naples. A diptych of King René and his wife by Froment is in the Louvre. There are two documented works by Froment: *The Raising of Lazarus* was painted in 1461 for a Florentine monastery, and *The Virgin in the Burning Bush* in 1476 for René I. The former provides evidence that Froment traveled to Italy. Froment's work shows some Flemish influence, transformed and assimilated into a personal style.

## FRANÇOIS GÉRARD                                                        1770-1837

*A successful portraitist who was the rival of David*

François Gérard was born in Rome in 1770, and in 1786 became a pupil of David. By 1795 his reputation as a portraitist was made, and rivaled that of David. Their former friendship deteriorated as David grew envious of Gérard's easy success. Gérard did not subscribe to David's ideals about the prime importance of history painting, and David angered Gérard by his slighting remarks on portraiture. Later, the two quarreled outright when the celebrated beauty Madame Récamier posed for Gérard before David's portrait of her was finished.

During the Empire, Gérard painted his only battlepiece, *The Battle of Austerlitz*, and some historical and mythological compositions to the glory of Napoleon. Change of regime did not affect him, and with the restoration of the Bourbon monarchy in 1814 he secured a court appointment and enjoyed a period of dazzling success, employing many assistants to help with his glossy portraits. He was ennobled by Louis XVIII. Gérard's portraits have considerable charm, and made him one of the most famous painters of the First Empire. His sketches are particularly lively; most of them are to be found at Versailles.

### HIS WORKS INCLUDE

Sacrifice of Jeroboam, 1752
*Paris, École des B-A.*

The Washerwoman, about 1761
*Amiens, Mus. de Picardie*

The High Priest Coresus Sacrificing himself to Save Callirrhoë, 1765
*Paris, Louvre*

The Fountain of Love, 1785
*London, Wallace Coll.*

L'Étude
*Paris, Louvre*

**See also pages 134, 135, 182, 183**

### HIS WORKS INCLUDE

The Raising of Lazarus, 1461
*Florence, Uffizi*

**See also page 93**

### HIS WORKS INCLUDE

Cupid and Psyche, 1789
*Paris, Louvre*

Portrait of Madame Regnault, 1789
*Paris, Louvre*

Portrait of Madame Récamier, 1802
*Paris, Mus. Carnavalet*

Portrait of Madame Visconti, 1810
*Paris, Louvre*

Corinne at Miseno, about 1819
*Lyons, Mus. des B-A.*

**See also page 141**

The Wounded Cuirassier
Leaving Battle, about 1814
*Paris, Louvre*

# THÉODORE GÉRICAULT 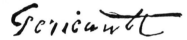 1791-1824

*One of the leaders of the Romantic school of painting*

Théodore Géricault was born in Rouen in 1791 of well-to-do parents, but moved to Paris as a child. He was a pupil of the fashionable equestrian painter Carle Vernet and of the Neoclassicist Baron Guérin. His early masterpiece, *The Officer of the Imperial Guard*, exhibited with great success at the 1812 Salon, shows that his true master was Gros.

Géricault was a passionate lover of horses, and most of his early paintings are of Napoleon's cavalrymen and their horses. In their realism, their drama, and their Rubens-like color, these pictures introduced to French painting the new flavor of Romanticism, and an alternative to the school of David.

In 1816 Géricault went to Italy after an unhappy love affair. He stayed there for a year copying the masters, especially Michelangelo, and studying antique art. On his return to France in 1817 he became completely absorbed in a painting to commemorate the Medusa affair, a naval disaster of which the liberals had made a political issue. Géricault spent weeks of preparation for this painting, *The Raft of the Medusa*. He conducted experiments with a model raft, interviewed the survivors, and studied corpses until it was said that his studio looked like a morgue. The picture made a profound impression at the 1819 Salon. In 1820 Géricault visited England, where he stayed for two years. There he made use of the opportunity to paint horse races, and put his art once more at the service of liberalism by making lithographs of the scenes of poverty that he saw in London. On his return to Paris

A Man Holding a Horse by the Bridle, 1814
*Paris, Louvre*

The Prince Regent as Colonel of Hussars
about 1821
*London, Wallace Coll.*

he was commissioned by a doctor to make a series of five facial studies of the insane, a task that evidently fascinated him and which he carried out with great sensitivity. Géricault's love of horses proved disastrous; he died after a riding accident when he was only 32.

A Horse Frightened by Lightning
London, N. G.

HIS WORKS INCLUDE

The Artillery Column, about 1812
Munich, Alte Pin.

Portrait of Eugène Delacroix,
about 1818
Rouen, Mus. des B-A.

The Kiln, 1821
Paris, Louvre

The Madman, about 1822
Ghent, Mus. des B-A.

The Coal Wagon (lithograph) 1822
Paris, Bibl. Nat., et al.

**See also pages 147, 148, 149, 188**

# FRANÇOIS GIRARDON

1628-1715

*The most classical sculptor of his time*

François Girardon, born at Troyes in 1628, worked in close collaboration with Charles Lebrun, who co-ordinated every aspect of the building and decoration of Louis XIV's palaces, particularly of Versailles. Sometime between 1645 and 1650 he was sent on a short visit to Rome.

On his return to Paris, Girardon attended the school of the Academy, becoming a member of the Academy in 1657. From 1663 he was working with Lebrun. In 1666 Girardon was given his first important commission, for a group of *Apollo and the Nymphs of Thetis*, to be placed in an alcove of the Grotto of Thetis at Versailles. The head of Apollo is closely modeled on that of the Apollo Belvedere, and the whole is a work of pure Classicism. The original grouping was unfortunately altered in the late 18th century. Girardon's other important work at Versailles is the *Rape of Persephone*, three entwined figures carved from one block. Although it is meant to be seen only from the front, this statue has also been moved into an open space.

Girardon continued to fulfil many other public and private commissions, one of the most remarkable being the monument to Richelieu of 1675-77. This, which stands in the Church of the Sorbonne, established the type of the free-standing altar tomb. Girardon worked on an equestrian statue of Louis XIV, also based on classical models, from 1683 to 1692. This stood in the Place Vendôme until the Revolution of 1789, when it was destroyed.

When Girardon died in 1715, on the same day as Louis XIV, his important work was long behind him. During the 1690's, taste had moved away from the Italianate classical manner of which he was such a successful exponent. He was the most typical sculptor of the Louis XIV–Versailles style.

Model for the Statue of Louis XIV
formerly in the Place Vendôme
about 1683
Paris, Louvre

HIS WORKS INCLUDE

Bust of Jérôme Bignon (marble)
about 1656
Paris, St. Nicolas-du-Chardonnet

Bathing Nymphs
(relief formerly gilded lead)
about 1670
Versailles, Château Park

Winter (marble) about 1675
Versailles, Château Park

**See also page 202**

## JEAN GOUJON active 1540-1562

*The dominant figure among French sculptors of the mid-16th century*

Nothing is known of the circumstances of the birth or of the career of Jean Goujon before 1540. In that year he carved the columns supporting the organ loft in the Church of St. Maclou at Rouen. These are the work of a mature artist who had almost certainly visited Rome. From payments made to him by the authorities of Rouen Cathedral, it is evident that Goujon was as much an architect as a sculptor. He was responsible for part of the tomb of Louis de Brézé, husband of Diane de Poitiers, in Rouen Cathedral.

His next commission was probably the decorations in the Château of Écouen. These are from a transitional period before his mature work in Paris. They include bas-reliefs of the four Apostles, direct forerunners of the figures on the rood screen of St. Germain l'Auxerrois. The central panel is a *Pietà* that shows the influence of Italian sculpture. The emphasis is on such decorative devices as the effect of close folds of drapery against a plain background rather than on the emotion of the subject.

Goujon's most famous sculptures belong to the middle years of the century. They are the decorations of the *Fountain of the Innocents*, and the figures executed in collaboration with Lescot at the Louvre between 1549 and 1553. The *Fountain*, completed between 1547 and 1549, is characterized by the patterning in the drapery, in the scales of the sea monsters, and in the designs of the shells on which the nymphs ride.

After 1562 Goujon's name disappeared from the royal accounts. He may have died in that year, or may have gone to Bologna, dying there about 1568; but his last years are very obscure. Goujon's œuvre was outstanding for its grace and harmony, and was the culmination of the Renaissance in France.

Nymphs of the Fountain of the Innocents, 1547-49
*Paris, Places des Innocents*

### HIS WORKS INCLUDE

Caryatids, about 1551
*Paris, Louvre*
The Tympanum (external doorway)
*Paris, Mus. Carnavalet*

**See also page 197**

Pietà, about 1545
*Paris, Louvre*

# JEAN BAPTISTE GREUZE

*A prolific painter of sentimental genre subjects*

Jean Baptiste Greuze was the son of a tiler in Tournus, in Burgundy. After a period of hack work for a picture-a-day painter in Lyons, he went to Paris, where he eventually secured the patronage of a wealthy dilettante, La Live de Jully. In 1755 La Live put on show Greuze's painting *The Father Explaining the Bible to his Children*. The picture went straight to the heart of a sentimental public, and set the tone for a profitable series—*The Village Betrothal, The Ungrateful Son, The Paralytic Attended by his Children*, and many more. They depended on their sentimental appeal for their success, but show Greuze's great technical ability. The subjects were in keeping with the contemporary love of moralizing and with the taste for rural subject matter that sprang up among devotees of the philosopher Jean Jacques Rousseau.

The philosopher Diderot was one of those who were enthusiastic. He exhorted Greuze, "This kind of painting appeals to me; it breathes morality... do not lose heart, friend Greuze! Preach morality and stick to your present path." Later, Diderot changed his opinion, saying simply, "I no longer like Greuze."

In 1769 Greuze offered an unimaginative and feebly executed painting of *Septimus Severus Reproaching his Son* in an attempt to gain admission to the Academy as a historical painter. So bad was the work and so objectionable was Greuze's character, that his fellow artists would accept him only as a painter of genre subjects—everyday scenes—then considered an inferior category. His vanity was gravely injured, and he withdrew from all further Salons, showing his work privately. His portraits were, for the most part, excellent, and his drawings have a freshness lacking in his finished compositions.

During the 1770's Greuze revived his flagging popularity with a series of paintings of pretty young girls, of which *The Broken Pitcher* is a famous example. The apparent innocence of the subjects is belied by their languorous eyes and rumpled clothing. Greuze's public remained enthusiastic.

The Revolution of 1789 ruined Greuze in spite of the considerable fortune he had amassed. The French dropped the cult of domestic virtue in favor of the civic virtue depicted by David. Greuze lingered on until 1805, executing a few charitable commissions, and comforted only by the devotion of his daughter.

Self-portrait
*Paris, Louvre*

*J. B. Greuze.*

HIS WORKS INCLUDE

The Father Explaining the Bible to his Children, 1755
*Leningrad, Hermitage*

The Village Betrothal, 1761
*Paris, Louvre*

The Paralytic Attended by his Children, 1763
*Leningrad, Hermitage*

Portrait of the Engraver Willie, 1763
*Paris, Mus. Jacquemart-André*

Boy with a Dog, 1769
*London, Wallace Coll.*

**See also pages 133, 182**

A Child with an Apple
*London, N. G.*

The Ungrateful Son, about 1765
*Paris, Louvre*

*The favorite pupil of the Neoclassic painter David*

Antoine Jean Gros was born in Paris in 1771 of artistic parents. He studied with David from 1785 until 1792. He failed to win the Prix de Rome, but went to Italy in 1794, working mainly in Genoa and Florence. In 1796 he met Napoleon, and for a short time was attached to his court. He followed the Italian campaign and joined the commission that selected works of art for removal to France.

Gros returned to Paris in 1800, and at the Salons of 1801 and 1802 exhibited large portraits of Napoleon. The general saw the usefulness of a painter who could glorify his regime, and commissioned a series of enormous pictures, of which *The Pesthouse at Jaffa* and *Napoleon at the Battle of Eylau* are the most celebrated. These, and the full-length portraits of Napoleon's generals, with their heroic bravado, modern subject matter and Rubenesque color caught the imagination of young artists like Géricault and Delacroix. They established for Gros his place as a precursor of both realist and romantic painting.

After the fall of Napoleon in 1815, Gros changed his allegiance to work for the Bourbon monarchs, but, lacking the inspiration of the Napoleonic age, his painting rapidly declined in quality. David, in exile, asked him to take charge of his pupils, and expected Gros to defend the Neoclassical style against the new Romanticism (with which Gros' natural sympathies would seem to lie). His late paintings, apart from portraits, are empty mythologies and funeral decorations, including the immense *Apotheosis of the Bourbons* (an *Apotheosis of Napoleon* when it had been commissioned in 1811) for the cupola of the Pantheon in Paris. Gros was ennobled by Charles X in 1824 for this painting. His last years however were tragic. Derisive criticism and an unhappy marriage led him eventually in 1835 to suicide by drowning in the Seine.

Self-portrait
*Versailles, Château*

*Gros*

HIS WORKS INCLUDE

The Battle of Nazareth, about 1801
*Nantes, Mus. des B-A.*

Portrait of General
Fournier-Sarlovèze, 1812
*Paris, Louvre*

Bonaparte Reviewing the Troops
*London, Wallace Coll.*

Salles des Antiquities Égyptiennes
(decorations) about 1830
*Paris, Louvre*

**See also pages 142, 143**

Napoleon at Arcola, 1796
*Versailles, Château*

Portrait of Christine Boyer,
about 1800   *Paris, Louvre*

# JEAN ANTOINE HOUDON

1741-1828

*An eminent 18th-century sculptor*

Jean Antoine Houdon was born at Versailles in 1741. His father later became care-taker at the École Royale des Élèves Protégés, the special school maintained by the Academy for its star pupils. Houdon attended this school from 1761, after working for a while as a pupil of Jean Baptiste Lemoyne, Jean Baptiste Pigalle, and Michel Ange Slodtz.

In 1764 Houdon won the Prix de Rome and went to Italy. He was more interest-ed in anatomy than in antiquity or the Baroque style. In Rome he made his name with the noble and simple statue of St. Bruno that stands in the Church of Santa Maria degli Angeli. He returned to Paris in 1769, where he became an Associate of the Academy. He presented his diploma work, *Morpheus*, in 1771, and was elected a full member in 1777.

Houdon, in the early part of his career, executed many commissions for the courts of Russia and Saxony, including funeral monuments and a statue of *Diana*. He is remembered chiefly for his strikingly alive portrait busts of many of the important people of his time. Among them was Benjamin Franklin who was in Paris in 1778 on a diplomatic mission. On the strength of this work, Houdon was asked to produce a statue of Washington, and in 1785 he visited America to begin it. It was completed in Paris in 1790, and shown at the 1792 Salon.

During the French Revolution Houdon only narrowly escaped imprisonment, but he continued to work under Napoleon. After 1814 he no longer undertook commissions. He was a professor at the Academy from 1805 until 1823, when ad-vancing senility compelled him to stop teaching. Houdon stood above the other sculptors of his time, and his Classicism equaled that of the architect Jacques Ange Gabriel. His style was outstanding for its simplicity and careful observation, its sense of balance and realistic precision.

St. Bruno, about 1768
*Rome, S. Maria degli Angeli*

# HOUDON.

Alexandre Brongniart
about 1780   *Paris, Louvre*

Voltaire, about 1784
*Paris, Comédie Française*

## HIS WORKS INCLUDE

Morpheus (marble) 1771
*Paris, Louvre*

Benjamin Franklin (marble) 1778
*New York, Met. Mus.*

Diana (marble) 1780
*Lisbon, Gulbenkian Foundation*

Bust of Voltaire (marble) 1781
*London, V. and A.*

Winter and Summer (marble) 1783
*Montpellier, Mus. Fabre*

Bust of Malesherbes (marble) 1784
*Paris, Louvre*

George Washington, 1790
*Richmond, Va., Capitol*

Napoleon, 1806
*Dijon, Mus. des B-A.*

**See also page 209**

55

## PAUL HUET                                                    1803-1869

*A Romantic landscape painter in oils and watercolor*

Paul Huet was born in Paris in 1803 and lived and worked there all his life. He studied at the École des Beaux-Arts from 1820, and was the pupil first of Antoine Jean Gros, the Romantic painter, and then of Baron Guérin. It was in the latter's studio that he met Delacroix, in 1822 or 1823.

Huet became an accomplished landscape painter, producing works with a strong emotional quality. His favorite motifs were dark, mysterious settings, with heavy skies and dramatic lighting. Huet's landscapes owe something to the influence of Constable and Bonington.

Huet also worked in the media of engraving and lithography. With a number of other artists, including Richard Bonington, Antoine Vernet, and the French architect Eugène Viollet-le-Duc, he collaborated in a series of lithographs illustrating "Voyages pittoresques et romantiques dans l'ancienne France," published between 1820 and 1828. In addition, he collaborated with Eugène Isabey and Ernest Meissonier in illustrating "Paul et Virginie," a celebrated novel by Bernardin de St. Pierre. Huet summed up his own work by defining it as "the expression of that secret communication which is established between man and nature when she penetrates him with her eloquent silence." He died in Paris in 1869.

**HIS WORKS INCLUDE**

The Park of St. Cloud on a Holiday, 1829
*Paris, Louvre*
Rouen in 1831, 1831
*Rouen, Mus. des B-A.*
Study of an Ox, about 1858
*Paris, Louvre*
Cottage in Normandy
*Paris, Louvre*

**See also page 190**

---

## JEAN AUGUSTE DOMINIQUE INGRES              1780-1867

*A leading advocate of Classicism, famous for his portraits*

Ingres was born in 1780 in Montauban in the south of France, where his father was an impecunious ornamental sculptor, painter, and drawing master. In 1791 he entered the Academy of Fine Arts at Toulouse, where his true talent became increasingly apparent. He worked for a while under Jean Briant, a landscape painter who wished Ingres to be one too, but Ingres, already an admirer of Raphael, realized that it was not the branch of painting for him. He left for Paris in 1797.

In Paris, Ingres entered David's studio and in 1801 won the Grand Prix de Rome with his painting *The Envoys from Agamemnon*. He could not leave France, however, because of the political crisis. While waiting for the situation to ease he painted mostly portraits. These included numerous portraits of Napoleon and of the Rivière family.

In 1806 he went to Rome, where he began to paint ambitious classical and historical pictures like *Jupiter and Thetis*. His work met with apathy from the public, and disapproval from the authorities in Paris. Ingres remained in Rome, earning a living from portrait drawings. A move to Florence in 1820 brought none of the hoped-for improvement in his circumstances. He continued to make small pencil portraits of English tourists for a living.

At last Ingres received a commission to paint a *Vow of Louis XIII* for the cathe-

Self-portrait, about 1800
*Chantilly, Mus. Condé*

INGRES

dral of Montauban. The picture, exhibited in the 1824 Salon, was widely praised and Ingres was showered with congratulations. He was commissioned to paint *The Martyrdom of St. Symphorian* for Autun Cathedral, and the *Apotheosis of Homer* for the ceiling of the new museum in the Louvre. For eight years he enjoyed his success. He was the acknowledged chief of Parisian painters, his studio was thronged, and he was kept hard at work teaching and fulfilling commissions.

In 1834, Ingres' popularity ended as suddenly as it had begun. When completed, *The Martyrdom of St. Symphorian* was received with anger and disgust by the Paris critics, who now preferred the Romantic paintings of Delacroix. Ingres resolved never to show his work in Paris again, and left at once for Rome to be the director of the French school there. The success of a later painting, *Stratonice*, made his return to Paris in 1841 a happier occasion. Ingres' last important commission was for a decorative scheme for the Château of Dampierre, but, disheartened by the death of his wife and the technical difficulties of mural painting, he abandoned the work in 1849. Another decorative work, the *Apotheosis of Napoleon I*, painted in 1853 for the Town Hall, was destroyed by fire in 1871.

Ingres also continued to paint portraits, religious subjects, nudes, and figure compositions, of which the most important is *The Turkish Bath*, completed in 1863. In 1855 on the occasion of a large retrospective exhibition at the Paris Universal Exhibition he was made a Grand Officer of the Legion of Honor. In his last years Ingres had a large number of pupils who continued to work in the classical tradition, in complete opposition to Delacroix and the Romantics. Ingres was made a senator in 1862. He died in January, 1867, after an exceptionally healthy and active old age.

*G. Wildenstein Ingres London, 1954*

La Source, about 1856
*Paris, Louvre*

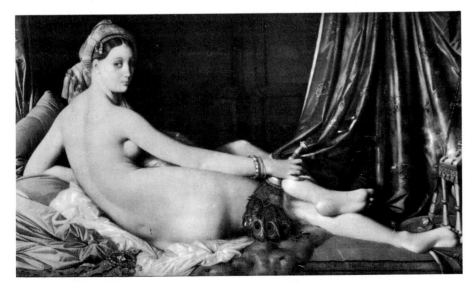

La Grande Odalisque, 1814
*Paris, Louvre*

57

**See also page 122**

*Lancret.*

# NICOLAS LANCRET                    1690-1743

*A painter of gay and charming court and garden scenes*

Nicolas Lancret was the son of a Paris coachman. His first master was that same Claude Gillot who had befriended Watteau. Lancret's work was essentially imitative. Watteau advised him to free himself from Gillot's influence and to study "that master of masters, nature." Lancret left Gillot, but only to transfer his allegiance to Watteau, whose manner he copied so faithfully that his work was often mistaken for Watteau's. This vexed Watteau, and led to an estrangement. Lancret continued to copy Watteau, and his work, though rather slight, is charming.

Childhood, from The Four Ages of Man
*London, N. G.*

The Turtle Doves
*Birmingham, England, Barber Inst.*

Self-portrait (detail)
*Versailles, Château*

*Largillierre*

# NICOLAS DE LARGILLIERRE            1656-1746

*The most fashionable portrait painter of his day*

Nicolas de Largillierre's parents moved from Paris to Antwerp soon after his birth in 1656, and so his training is unique among French painters. At an early age he was apprenticed to a painter of still-life and peasant scenes, Antoine Goubaud, and in 1672 was received as a master by the guild of Antwerp. In 1674 he went to London where he entered the studio of the portrait painter Peter Lely, for whom he painted draperies and still-life accessories. By 1682, he felt ready to establish himself as a painter in his own right. He went to Paris, and settled there for the rest of his long life, only revisiting England once in 1685 to paint portraits of James II and Mary of Modena. These are now lost.

In 1684 Largillierre became a member of the Academy, and his diploma painting was a portrait of Charles Lebrun. This work established the type of the "state portrait" of a painter. It displays Lebrun in an attitude suitable to his dignity and importance surrounded by the tools symbolic of his art and achievement. Yet Largillierre, with his Flemish and English training, was to help to replace the strict academic style by a freer and more individual manner of painting.

Largillierre spent the rest of his life in increasing prosperity, painting portraits of rich Parisian bourgeois either individually or with their families, set amid the flurrying silks, rich draperies, and Negro servants that bear witness to their wealth.

### HIS WORKS INCLUDE

Portrait of Charles Lebrun, 1684
*Paris, Louvre*

The Échevins of Paris before
Ste. Geneviève, 1696
*Paris, St. Étienne-du-Mont*

La Belle Strasbourgeoise, 1703
*Strasbourg, Mus. des B-A.*

**See also page 115**

## GEORGES DE LA TOUR                           1593-1652

*A painter of simple yet deeply moving religious pictures*

Georges de La Tour was born in 1593 at Vic-sur-Seille in the Duchy of Lorraine, where he spent the whole of his life. By 1620 he was established as a successful and wealthy master in Lunéville, one of the chief towns of the duchy. Although in 1623 the Duke of Lorraine commissioned him for two works, his commissions came mainly from the wealthy bourgeois. A *St. Sebastian* by La Tour may have been owned by Louis XIII, but even if this is true, the king probably valued it more for the saint's protection against the plague than as a work of art.

La Tour's paintings became increasingly simple and calm in their composition. Mainly of religious subjects, they are often lit only by a single torch. The drawing is somewhat generalized but this is compensated for by the power of his composition. His early works, scenes of everyday life, were executed in daylight, with no

Christ and St. Joseph
*Paris, Louvre*

Mary Magdalene
*Paris, Louvre*

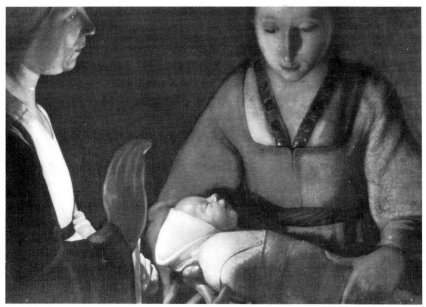

The Newborn Child (detail)
*Rennes, Mus.*

## HIS WORKS INCLUDE

The Fortune Teller
*New York, Met. Mus.*

The Viol Player
*Nantes, Mus. des B-A.*

The Angel Appearing to St. Joseph
*Nantes, Mus. des B-A.*

The Cheat
*Paris, coll. Pierre Landry*

The Adoration of the Shepherds
*Paris, Louvre*

**See also pages 102, 103**

strong contrasts of tone. After 1630 most of La Tour's paintings were nocturnal religious scenes, in which the lighting is artificial.

Many influences have been traced in La Tour's work, notably that of Caravaggio, but the mystical quality of his imagination eludes such analysis. His fame was confined to Lorraine in his lifetime, and for many years his identity was unknown. His works were attributed to Vermeer and Velázquez among others; evidently their quality was recognized even while their authorship remained obscure.

*S. M. Furness   Georges de La Tour of Lorraine   London, 1949*

---

Self-portrait
*Paris, Louvre*

## MAURICE QUENTIN DE LATOUR                    1704-1788

*The most accomplished of portraitists to work in pastel*

Maurice Quentin de Latour was born in 1704 in northeastern France, where his father was cantor to the collegiate church of St. Quentin. At the age of 15 he went to Paris, where he worked under a Dutch master.

In 1724 Latour attended the Congress of Cambrai, a magnificent diplomatic and social occasion, where the various ambassadors vied with one another in displays of wealth and taste. Latour was lucky; his facility in catching a likeness made his work wildly fashionable, and the English ambassador offered him lodging in London if he would go there. He accepted the offer and went to London, where his patron's position ensured his success.

On his return to Paris, Latour began to use pastels rather than oils for his portraits. Louis de Boulogne, the chief court painter, gave him some severe but sound advice: "Young man, you should draw, you should keep on drawing." Latour took his counsel and entered upon two years devoted entirely to drawing. This period of valuable self-development consolidated his almost too immediate success, and his drawings and sketches are often superior to his more finished works.

Latour had become a member of the Academy in 1737, but so complete was his fashionable dominance that in 1749 the Academy closed its doors to pastellists, saying that "M. de Latour has so developed the art of pastel as to make us fear that he may provoke a distaste for oil painting." The only opposition he met was slight; some critics accused him of spoiling the freshness of his work by excessive retouching.

## HIS WORKS INCLUDE

Portrait of Madame Leczinska
(pastel) about 1744
*Paris, Louvre*

Portrait of Henry Dawkins (pastel)
about 1750
*London, N. G.*

Portrait of d'Alembert (pastel) 1753
*Paris, Louvre*

Portrait of Madame de Pompadour
(pastel) 1755
*Paris, Louvre*

Portrait of Mademoiselle d'Angeville
(drawing)
*Paris, Louvre*

The largest collection of de Latour's pastels and sketches are in the Maurice Quentin de Latour Museum, Saint-Quentin.

**See also page 129**

Success did not improve Latour's character. Always self-assertive, his rudeness extended even to Louis XV and his all-powerful mistress, Madame de Pompadour. He was mean and his prices were exorbitant. Nevertheless, society continued to humor him, to employ him and to pay him.

From 1770 onwards he began to show signs of increasing mental weakness. In 1784 he returned to St. Quentin, where he fell into a childish senility before he died in 1788. According to the terms of Latour's will, his brother bequeathed to the city of St. Quentin all the works of art left to him by Latour, and it is there that the largest collection of his pastels and studies is to be seen.

# CHARLES LEBRUN

*The dictator of the art and taste of his time*

Charles Lebrun was born in Paris in 1619 and received his first training from Simon Vouet. He went to Italy in 1642 and stayed there for four years. During this time he studied under Poussin; and he was also influenced by the contemporary Roman decorative painters. When he returned to Paris in 1646 he was immediately given commissions for decorative and religious paintings. In the 1650's Lebrun worked in the Hôtel Lambert, the town house of Jean Baptiste Lambert, with Le Vau. Here he painted a huge ceiling decoration depicting the story of Hercules, which was the most complicated example of Baroque illusionism executed in France at that time. In the same decade he worked for Nicolas Fouquet at Vaux-le-Vicomte. These decorations combined stucco, gilding, and painting, and show the influence of Pietro da Cortona's decorations in the Pitti Palace, Florence. In the Gallery of Apollo at the Louvre Lebrun evolved the style he was later to use in Louis XIV's first apartments at Versailles, in which painting and sculpture are employed in a clear and straightforward fashion.

With the co-operation of the king's minister, Jean Baptiste Colbert, Lebrun reorganized the French Academy. In 1661 he carried out his first commission for the king, *The Tent of Darius*. This established his position with the monarch and led to his becoming the arbiter of artistic taste. He retained his supremacy until Colbert's death in 1683, after which Lebrun's rival Pierre Mignard gained the upper hand. By this time Lebrun had created the machinery that was devoted to the glorification of the king, and that laid down strict rules for style and subject matter in painting. He produced a treatise on the expression of the passions, and put the greatest emphasis on the laws of reason.

In 1663 Lebrun was also made a director of the Gobelins tapestry factory, which he used to help standardize the style of art all over France. He worked with Le Vau and Claude Perrault on the architecture of the Louvre in 1667, after Bernini's designs had been rejected. From 1671 to 1681 Lebrun directed the decorations for the Grands Appartements at Versailles, working with Jules Hardouin Mansart on the Hall of Mirrors, the Salon de la Guerre, and the Salon de la Paix. The Grands Appartements were treated in a fashion similar to the Gallery of Apollo, but included hall panels with illusionist decoration.

In his last years Lebrun was set aside in favor of his rival Mignard, though the king continued to commission a variety of small easel paintings from him. Lebrun had been highly thought of by his contemporaries and indeed had held a position of unrivaled importance. He had played an impressive role in the uniform excellence of the visual arts during the reign of Louis XIV. Lebrun's importance cannot be overestimated for it was certainly due to him, with the king and Colbert, that France was to take over from Italy supremacy in the field of art in the following century.

Self-portrait
*Florence, Uffizi*

## CLB

### HIS WORKS INCLUDE

Hercules and Horses of Diomedes,
about 1640
*Nottingham, England, Art Gall.*

The Tent of Darius, 1661
*Paris, Louvre*

The Story of Alexander (series of 4)
about 1673
*Paris, Louvre*

Louis XIV Adoring the Risen Christ,
about 1676
*Lyons, Mus. des B-A.*

The Descent from the Cross,
about 1679
*Rennes, Mus. de Rennes*

**See also pages 114, 177**

The Marquise de Brinvilliers
before her Execution
*Paris, Bibl. Nat.*

## JEAN BAPTISTE LEMOYNE

1704-1778

*A Rococo sculptor*

## HIS WORKS INCLUDE

Bust of Jacques Ange Gabriel
(marble) about 1760
*Paris, Louvre*

Bust of Chancelier Maupeou, 1768
*Paris, Mus. Jacquemart-André*

Bust of Louis XV (marble) 1769
*Paris, Louvre*

Bust of Marie Antoinette (marble)
1771
*Vienna, Kunsthist. Mus.*

Bust of Mademoiselle d'Angeville
(marble) 1771
*Paris, Comédie Française*

**See also page 205**

Jean Baptiste Lemoyne was the son of a sculptor who was one of the team of artists working at Versailles. In 1725 he won the Prix de Rome, but was never able to make the journey to Italy. *The Baptism of Christ*, done for the Church of St. Roch in Paris in 1731, gained him general recognition, but he is best known for his portrait busts. These, like the series of quick pastel portraits drawn by Lemoyne's friend and contemporary Latour, represent the notable people of the time—courtiers and scholars, great ladies and actresses. Lemoyne was appointed sculptor to the king by Louis XV, and he was a celebrated teacher.

---

## ANTOINE LE NAIN
## LOUIS    LE NAIN
## MATHIEU LE NAIN

about 1588-1648<br>about 1593-1648<br>about 1607-1677

*Three brothers who painted everyday life among poor people*

LOUIS LE NAIN
The Adoration of the Shepherds
(detail)   *London, N. G.*

## THEIR WORKS INCLUDE

ANTOINE LE NAIN
Family Reunion
*Paris, Louvre*

LOUIS LE NAIN
The Cart
*Paris, Louvre*

MATHIEU LE NAIN
Corps de Garde, 1643
*Paris, Baronne de Berckheim Coll.*

**See also pages 99, 100, 101**

The Le Nain brothers were all painters born at Laon in northeastern France. About 15 signed pictures by them survive, but as the signature is always simply "Le Nain" and all are dated before 1638, there is no definite evidence for assigning any of them to one or other of the brothers. On occasion they may have collaborated. However, the pictures are usually divided into three main groups, according to the characteristics of each of the brothers.

Antoine, the eldest, moved to Paris in 1629, to become master painter to the Abbey of Saint-Germain-des-Prés. He was said by a contemporary to excel "in miniatures and portraits in small." To him are attributed small pictures painted on copper. They mostly show family groups, either bourgeois or peasant, naively arranged and painted in strong, pure color.

Louis was much the best artist of the three. He was in Paris by 1630. His paintings are larger than Antoine's and subdued in color, while their almost classical composition makes it seem likely that he visited Rome. They are mainly scenes of peasant life, neither satirized nor idealized, but painted with observant sympathy.

The youngest brother, Mathieu, seems to have had a quite different character. In 1633 he became master painter to the city of Paris and made a successful career for himself. He was a lieutenant in the city militia and was made a chevalier, and his paintings reflect this side of life. Of the pictures attributed to him the masterpiece is the *Corps de Garde*, which shows a party of officers drinking at a table. The scene is candlelit and in its full and vigorous style reflects the influence of Caravaggio.

# EUSTACHE LE SUEUR

*An artist drawn toward a classical style dependent on Raphael*

A Parisian by birth, Eustache Le Sueur entered Simon Vouet's studio in 1632. The master passed a commission for some tapestry designs on to his pupil, and these, completed in about 1637, are Le Sueur's earliest known works. They show that Le Sueur had learned Vouet's manner well, but had as yet established no independent style.

In about 1646 Le Sueur embarked upon his first major work, the decoration of the Cabinet de l'Amour at the Hôtel Lambert with a history of Cupid. In this work a certain lightness of drawing and calmness of composition distinguish his work from that of Vouet. This independence increases in Le Sueur's paintings for the Cabinet des Muses.

Although he never went to Rome, Le Sueur was drawn to the classical style and studied Raphael in engravings. Tradition has it that he came to know Poussin well in the two years that Poussin spent in Paris from 1640 to 1642. This is probably untrue, though Le Sueur's work of the 1640's shows Poussin's influence, especially his St. Bruno series. This series, painted for the Charterhouse in Paris about 1648, is his best work. Added to the significant and classical composition learned from Poussin is an impression of real religious feeling.

Before he died Le Sueur's work was deteriorating into an uninspired copying of Raphael. He was much admired in his own day, and in the 18th century.

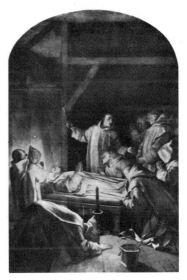

St. Bruno, about 1648
*Paris, Louvre*

*Le Sueur.*

The Three Muses (detail) about 1649
*Paris, Louvre*

## HIS WORKS INCLUDE

Poliphilus before Queen Eleutherilida, about 1637
*Rouen, Mus. des B-A.*

The Presentation of the Virgin, 1640-45
*Leningrad, Hermitage*

The Angel Leaving Tobias, about 1650
*Grenoble, Mus. des B-A.*

St. Gervasius and St. Protasius, about 1650
*Paris, Louvre*

Christ and Mary Magdalen, 1651
*Paris, Louvre*

St. Sebastian, about 1655
*Tours, Mus. des B-A.*

**See also pages 112, 176**

February, about 1416
*Chantilly, Mus. Condé*

THEIR WORKS INCLUDE

Très Riches Heures du Duc de Berri
1411-16 (unfinished)
*Chantilly, Mus. Condé*
Belles Heures du Duc de Berri
*New York, Met. Mus., Cloisters*

**See also page 85**

Paradise
*Chantilly, Mus. Condé*

# POL DE LIMBOURG
# HENNEQUIN DE LIMBOURG
# HERMANN DE LIMBOURG

*Miniaturists at the court of the Duke of Berri at the beginning of the 15th century*

The brothers Pol, Hennequin and Hermann de Limbourg were related to the painter Jehan Malouel. An early mention of them occurs in the accounts of the Duchy of Burgundy for 1402. They were born in the Netherlands, were apprenticed to a Flemish goldsmith in Paris, and were active in the service of the dukes of Burgundy and Berri. Pol had painted the *Breviary of Jean Sans Peur* while he was in Burgundy. The most famous work of the Limbourgs is the *Très Riches Heures du Duc de Berri*, which they worked on from 1411 onwards, and which was finished after their deaths. This manuscript, which is a kind of calendar, represents the highest achievement of the International Gothic style, and is remarkable for its treatment of landscape. The castles represented in the backgrounds can be identified with actual buildings, and the scenes represent contemporary life. The atmosphere of the Berri court is reflected in their work. Pol de Limbourg was not only court painter, but also valet de chambre to the duke.

John, Duke of Berri, was the brother of Charles V and of Philip the Bold, Duke of Burgundy. He made his court a center of the arts, and employed the best artists of the day. It is possible that Pol de Limbourg worked on the manuscript known as the *Belles Heures*, for it was probably produced between 1402 and 1413, and he is known to have been employed by the duke by 1409.

Another artist at the court was the sculptor, architect, and painter André Beauneveu from Valenciennes. He lived at Bourges, and was consulted by the duke in all matters connected with the arts. He may have been responsible for many of the decorations of the Sainte Chapelle at Bourges, and of the Château of Mehun-sur-Yèvre. He is almost certainly responsible for the grisaille miniatures at the beginning of a psalter made for the Duke of Berri, on which he was working in 1402. Beauneveu died some time before 1413, but he had influenced painting over a large area of northern Europe, from Bourges to Poitiers, and even in Flanders and the Rhineland.

The painter who preceded the Limbourg brothers in the service of the Duke of Berri was Jacquemart de Hesdin. He must have been responsible for many of the illuminations in the *Grandes Heures du Duc de Berri*, and, with Jan van Eyck, was probably one of the painters employed on the *Belles Heures* illuminations.

## SIMON MARMION

active 1449-1489

*A painter and miniaturist of the Franco-Flemish School*

Very little is known for certain about the life of the early French painter Simon Marmion. He was born either in Amiens or Valenciennes, and spent his life working in these two towns and at Tournai.

Marmion's main work, an altarpiece of originally 12 panels, representing the life of St. Bertin, was executed for the Abbey of Saint-Omer between 1454 and 1459. The panels, which are now dispersed, show an acute sense of reality. He also painted illuminated manuscripts of great delicacy in design and color.

HIS WORKS INCLUDE
Attrib. to SIMON MARMION
The Invention of the True Cross, about 1460
*Paris, Louvre*
The Virgin and Child
*Amsterdam, Rijksmus.*
Pontifical of the Église de Sens (manuscript)
*Brussels, Bibl. Royale*

**See also page 92**

## MASTER OF THE AIX ANNUNCIATION

active about 1400-50

*An anonymous 15th-century painter who produced a key work of French art*

Before 1445 a triptych of the *Annunciation* flanked by two prophets was placed in the Cathedral of Aix-en-Provence. The central portion is now in the Church of La Madeleine, but the wings are dispersed, one being in Brussels and the other, in two parts, in Holland. It is not possible to identify the painter of this work, which shows a mixture of styles and influences.

The artist was probably from the entourage of painters of René I, Duke of Anjou and Lorraine and King of Naples, and does show some affinities with the King René Master. The influence of the Burgundian painters is evident, and the *Annunciation* shows certain parallels to Conrad Witz, and even to Antonio Niccolò Colantonio, a Neapolitan master, which suggests that the painter was widely traveled. The center panel depicts an interior of a French cathedral. The pulpit is remarkably like that in a drawing of *St. Jerome in his Study* by Pol de Limbourg. The figures have some similarity to the work of Jean Fouquet, and the sculpture of Claus Sluter.

Isaiah, from the triptych of
The Annunciation (detail) about 1445
*Rotterdam, Boymans-van Beuningen*

HIS WORKS INCLUDE
Jeremiah, completed 1445
*Brussels, Mus. Royaux des B-A.*

**See also page 91**

## MASTER OF MOULINS

active about 1480-1499

*An unknown artist responsible for a famous triptych*

The Master of the Moulins triptych has been identified with many painters, including Jean Perréal and Jean Bourdichon, but his true name remains a mystery. Whoever he was, he was evidently influenced by the Flemish painter Hugo van der Goes. The triptych of *The Madonna and Child with Angels* was placed in Moulins Cathedral in about 1498 or 1499. There are other works attributed to the hand of this unknown artist. He seems to have been active mainly at the Bourbon court at Moulins, and ranks among the best French painters of the end of the 15th century.

HIS WORKS INCLUDE
The Nativity with Cardinal Jean Rolin as Donor, about 1480
*Autun, Mus. des B-A.*
The Madonna and Child with Four Angels
*Brussels, Mus. Royaux des B-A.*
St. Maurice and a Donor
*Glasgow, Art Gall.*

**See also pages 94, 163**

## HIS WORKS INCLUDE

Self-portrait (chalk drawing)
before 1635
*Abbeville, Mus. des B-A.*

Portrait of Pierre Séguier (drawing)
1639
*Leningrad, Hermitage*

Portrait of Philippe d'Orléans as a
Child (drawing) about 1655
*Leningrad, Hermitage*

Éditions du Louvre
(engravings of well-known pictures)
*Paris, Bibl. Nat.*

**See also page 172**

## CLAUDE MELLAN

1598-1688

*An engraver of great technical ability*

Claude Mellan was born in Abbeville in 1598, but went to live in Paris while still young. His father was a coppersmith, and Mellan began his career by working on commercial engravings. His aptitude for engraving was noticed by a nobleman called Peiresc, who sent him to Rome, where he trained with Simon Vouet. During this period Mellan invented a new process of engraving, in which a varied, unbroken line was used.

When he returned to France this new development was much appreciated, and led to his appointment by Louis XIV as Engraver in Ordinary, the award of a pension, and lodging in the Louvre. For his patron Peiresc, Mellan carried out a series of engravings of well-known pictures, now called the *Éditions du Louvre*, in this new technique. For the rest of his life he devoted a great deal of time to perfecting methods of engraving.

Although he was not so well known for his painting, Mellan possessed considerable ability in this art. He died in Paris in 1688 after a long and successful career.

---

Self-portrait
*Paris, Louvre*

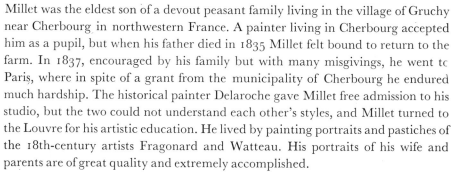

## JEAN FRANÇOIS MILLET

1814-1875

*An artist famous for his simple, solid paintings of peasants*

Millet was the eldest son of a devout peasant family living in the village of Gruchy near Cherbourg in northwestern France. A painter living in Cherbourg accepted him as a pupil, but when his father died in 1835 Millet felt bound to return to the farm. In 1837, encouraged by his family but with many misgivings, he went to Paris, where in spite of a grant from the municipality of Cherbourg he endured much hardship. The historical painter Delaroche gave Millet free admission to his studio, but the two could not understand each other's styles, and Millet turned to the Louvre for his artistic education. He lived by painting portraits and pastiches of the 18th-century artists Fragonard and Watteau. His portraits of his wife and parents are of great quality and extremely accomplished.

In 1844 two of Millet's works attracted attention at the Salon, but he was no longer in Paris, having gone back to Cherbourg on the death of his wife. He worked at Le Havre for a year, remarried, and returned to Paris. At this time he was painting mainly erotic, sensuous nudes in the manner of Correggio, sometimes given respectability by such titles as *Susanna and the Elders*.

Then in 1848 came a dramatic change of subject and style, which was eventually to bring Millet great public success. *The Winnower*, shown at the 1848 Salon, was bought by the State, and on the proceeds Millet left Paris for Barbizon, where he lived for the rest of his life in a three-roomed cottage. With Théodore Rousseau and Diaz de la Peña, Millet formed the core of the so-called Barbizon group of painters, who aimed at an exact and unromanticized picture of rural life.

After 1860, Millet's fame spread and his income increased. His paintings

The Woodcutters
*London, V. and A.*

The Whisper, about 1846
*London, N. G.*

### HIS WORKS INCLUDE

Mademoiselle Ono, about 1840
*Cherbourg, Mus. des B-A.*

The Winnower, 1848
*Paris, Louvre*

Quarrymen, about 1849
*Toledo, Ohio, Mus. of Art*

Sheaf Binders, 1850
*Paris, Louvre*

Spring, 1863-73
*Paris, Louvre*

**See also pages 157, 191**

The Angelus, 1859
*Paris, Louvre*

The Bathers
*Lille, Mus. des B-A.*

exhibited a sincere and solid quality, with simple but effective composition, and colors reflecting earth tones, and his drawings had great vitality and directness. He aroused some social controversy because he showed rural life in realistic rather than romantic fashion. In 1867 he received the ribbon of the Legion of Honor, but his health was badly undermined by grief at the death of his friend Théodore Rousseau. He lived until January, 1875.

## ROBERT NANTEUIL 1623-1678

*An eminent 17th-century portrait engraver*

Mazarin in his Study
*Paris, Bibl. Nat.*

### HIS WORKS INCLUDE

Portrait of Anne of Austria
(engraving) 1666
*Paris, Bibl. Nat., et al.*

Portrait of Madame de Sévigné
(pastel) about 1671
*Paris, Mus. Carnavalet*

**See also page 178**

Robert Nanteuil, who continued in his work the traditions of late Mannerism, produced engravings of technical excellence. He was born in Reims in 1623, but went to Paris, where he became one of the most illustrious men of his age.

Nanteuil worked as an engraver, draftsman, and pastelist. He engraved numerous portrait heads after Philippe de Champaigne. His engraved portraits from life showed strong powers of observation, and he is known to have made at least 244 of them. Among his sitters were Louis XIV, Anne of Austria, Cardinal Mazarin, and the king's minister Colbert. He worked in varied media, which included pencil, sanguine, and pen.

When Nanteuil became overburdened with work he was forced to employ a large number of assistants, and to draw only the faces of his subjects. He became one of the masters of the print in the 17th century, and he established the medium of engraving among the accepted liberal arts. His works provide the most detailed record in existence of the important figures of the 17th century.

## JEAN MARC NATTIER 1685-1766

*A portrait painter at the court of Louis XV*

### HIS WORKS INCLUDE

Portrait of Mademoiselle de
Clermont, 1733
*London, Wallace Coll.*

Portrait of Menon Balletti, 1757
*London, N. G.*

Portrait of Madame Adelaide
de France, about 1758
*Paris, Louvre*

Series of portraits of
Louis XV's Daughters, 1740-61
*Versailles, Mus.*

**See also page 130**

Born the son of a painter in Paris, Jean Marc Nattier had early success. At the age of 15 he won the first prize of the Academy. He rejected the offer of a post in the Academy of Rome, and was engaged to draw the Rubens decorations in the Luxembourg Palace for engravings.

In 1715 Nattier went to Amsterdam at the command of the Czar and painted portraits and history pictures for the Russian royal family. These portraits established his reputation, and although he lost his fortune in the speculations of the Scotsman John Law, he soon recouped it as the most fashionable painter of the ladies of Louis XV's court. He painted them in diaphanous disguise as Greek goddesses, and did not hesitate to flatter them. The result is that, in spite of his very real talent, his paintings all too often seem the dead records of a bygone mode of beauty. Nattier had very great success, but his fashionable popularity passed, and the vogue for his work died before he did.

# JEAN BAPTISTE OUDRY

*An artist renowned for his paintings of animals and his tapestry designs*

Jean Baptiste Oudry was born in Paris, the son of a gilder and art dealer, on March 17, 1686. As a young man he was the pupil of his father, of Michel Serre, and of Nicolas de Largillierre, through whom he made useful connections. He became a successful portrait painter and designer of historical scenes. He included among his sitters Peter the Great of Russia.

In 1719 Oudry was elected to the Academy, and began to specialize in landscape and animal painting. In 1722 he exhibited a hunting scene which so pleased the king that by 1730 he was the official painter of the king's hunt and favorite dogs. Oudry continued the tradition of Alexandre Desportes, who also painted hunting scenes and was influenced by Dutch and Flemish art.

The most important aspect of Oudry's work was his supervision of the Gobelins and the Beauvais tapestry manufactories. In 1726 Oudry was appointed designer to the Beauvais works, which he saved from ruin, and he agreed to supply six paintings suitable for tapestries every three years. He was appointed director in 1734, and two years later he was also given the supervision of a Gobelins tapestry made to record Louis XV's hunting parties, for which he had prepared the cartoons. He was connected with other works for the Gobelins factory between 1733 and 1735. Many tapestries were made from Oudry's designs, the subjects ranging from hunting scenes and animals in landscapes to illustrations of Ovid and Molière. His ideas revolutionized the technique of tapestry manufacture, for he insisted on the faithful reproduction of all the subtle shades and every detail of a painting. He commissioned the work of good contemporary artists, such as Boucher and Charles Natoire. His influence changed the style of tapestry decoration from the grandiose scenes of Louis XIV's reign to those of small size and delicate coloring, which he employed to harmonize with the new, light style of interior decoration.

Still-life
*Cambridge, Mass., Fogg Art Mus.*

*J B Oudry.*

HIS WORKS INCLUDE

The Dead Roe, 1721
*London, Wallace Coll.*

Fox in the Farmyard, 1748
*London, Wallace Coll.*

The Farm, 1750
*Paris, Louvre*

**See also page 121**

The Wolf Hunt
*Paris, Louvre*

A Hawk Attacking Wild Duck
*London, Wallace Coll.*

## JEAN BAPTISTE JOSEPH PATER 1695-1736

*A devoted imitator of Watteau*

*JB Pater*

Jean Baptiste Pater was born in Valenciennes, the son of a sculptor. He became Watteau's pupil, but the two quarreled and parted within a few months. Just before his death, Watteau repented of his irritability, and sent for Pater to give him a few last lessons. Pater painted theatrical scenes and *fêtes galantes* in his master's style for the rest of his life. Goaded by a dread of falling ill in poverty, he worked unceasingly to amass a considerable fortune but died, worn out, at the early age of 40.

Fête in a Park
*London, Wallace Coll.*

Blind Man's Buff
*London, Wallace Coll.*

## JEAN BAPTISTE PERRONNEAU 1715-1783

*Perronneau*

*A portraitist who caught the fancy of his time*

Born in Paris in 1715, Jean Baptiste Perronneau studied first under Charles Natoire and Laurent Cars. He worked for a time as an engraver, but from 1744 he began to make portraits in oil and paste. In 1753 he was nominated a full member of the Academy.

As a fashionable portrait painter, he was Maurice Quentin de Latour's only rival. In spite of their brilliant color, his portraits are more sincere and lively than the glossy productions of Latour. From about 1755, Perronneau traveled widely, fulfilling commissions in Holland, England, Italy, and provincial France. He was most successful in Holland, where he returned frequently and where he died.

## JEAN BAPTISTE PIGALLE

1714-1785

*A sculptor who gained the favor of Madame de Pompadour*

Born in Paris in 1714, Jean Baptiste Pigalle became a pupil of Jean Baptiste Lemoyne. He entered the competition for the Prix de Rome, but, when he failed, he traveled to Rome at his own expense in 1763. He stayed there for three years, enduring near starvation.

After his return to Paris in 1739 Pigalle won the favor of Madame de Pompadour, and for her he carved allegorical statues such as the *Love and Friendship* of 1758. Between 1753 and 1756 he worked on the tomb of the Maréchal de Saxe in the Church of St. Thomas in Strasbourg, and in 1776 he did a nude statue of Voltaire for the Institut de France. Pigalle's other great work was the base for Edmé Bouchardon's equestrian statue of Louis XV. The statue itself was destroyed in the Revolution of 1789, but the base is still preserved in the Place Royale at Reims. His style was notable for its vigor, and was in turn epic, realistic, and graceful.

### HIS WORKS INCLUDE

The Madonna and Child (marble) about 1748
*Paris, St. Sulpice*

Child with a Cage (marble) 1749
*Paris, Louvre*

Love and Friendship (marble) 1758
*Paris, Louvre*

Bust of Diderot (bronze) 1777
*Paris, Louvre*

**See also page 207**

---

## GERMAIN PILON

about 1535-1590

*A sculptor of the second half of the 16th century*

Germain Pilon was born in Paris in the mid 1530's. By 1560 he was working under Primaticcio on the monument for Henry II's heart. The three graces who support the casket are in the Mannerist style; they have the elegant and elongated limbs of Primaticcio's stucco decorations and paintings at Fontainebleau. In 1558 he received payment for eight statues for the tomb of Francis I, but these are no longer in existence.

Between 1563 and 1570 Pilon worked on the tomb of Henry II and Catherine de' Medici in the Abbey Church of St. Denis near Paris. Its bronze figures of the four virtues are in Pilon's style, but the figures of the king and queen kneeling on the top of the tomb are realistic in the French tradition for such figures, though they have a greater freedom than most. In the naked corpses within the tomb the naturalism is intensified, not by such gruesome details as the embalming stitches that are sometimes shown, but by the completely abandoned attitudes of death.

During the 1570's Pilon produced a series of portrait busts and medals, including a bust of Charles IX, which show that Pilon must have known the works of contemporary Italian sculptors. In the 1580's he was responsible for two sets of sculptures. One of these was the tombs of the Birague family, which were badly damaged during the 18th century. All that remain are the bronze kneeling figures of Cardinal Birague, the recumbent figure of his wife in marble, and the bas-relief of her corpse from the side of the sarcophagus. This last represents a return to the Middle Ages in its emaciated, almost skeletal appearance. The same pathetic aspect of death, but not the same grimness, is found in Pilon's bronze relief of *The Deposition*, now in the Louvre.

Pilon's later style was too personal to be emulated, but his early manner was a powerful influence on French sculpture into the 17th century.

Henry II, from the Tomb of Henry II and Catherine de' Medici, 1563-70
*Paris, St. Denis*

### HIS WORKS INCLUDE

Monument to the Heart of Henry II (marble) 1560
*Paris, Louvre*

Bust of Charles IX (marble)
*Paris, Louvre*

The Birague Tombs (fragments) (bronze) about 1583
*Paris, Louvre*

The Resurrection (fragments) about 1583
*Paris, Louvre*

The Virgin (marble) 1580-85
*Paris, Louvre*

**See also page 198**

# NICOLAS POUSSIN 1594-1665

*A painter whose work represents the supreme expression of French Classicism*

In 1612 Nicolas Poussin, a farmer's son, made his way from his home, near Les Andelys in Normandy, to Paris, intent on furthering his ambition to become a painter. He had been fired with this resolve by Quentin Varin, a painter who had worked for a time on altarpieces in Les Andelys. Little is known of Poussin's early years in Paris. By 1621, however, he was under the patronage of the Italian Marino, court poet of Maria de' Medici, the queen mother, and he worked with Philippe de Champaigne on the decorations for her Luxembourg Palace in Paris.

Encouraged and assisted by Marino, Poussin traveled to Rome in 1624 after two abortive attempts and many hardships. In the studio of Domenichino his genius was fully awakened. After five years of experimental work, he was commissioned in 1628 to execute an altarpiece for St. Peter's, but *The Martyrdom of St. Erasmus* that he painted was not a success. His early works (those before 1632) indicate that he had come into direct contact with Roman Baroque painting.

His failure and the severe illness that Poussin suffered at about this time were a turning point in his life. Afterwards he abandoned the search for public commissions for churches and palaces, and painted only relatively small pictures. He became dependent upon a small circle of intellectuals headed by Cassiano del Pozzo, a generous and scholarly man, whose life and resources were devoted to the study of antiquity. Pozzo commissioned artists, Poussin among them, to draw for his records every relic of Imperial Rome that was unearthed.

The influence of these friends caused Poussin to neglect religious subjects in

Self-portrait, 1650
*Paris, Louvre*

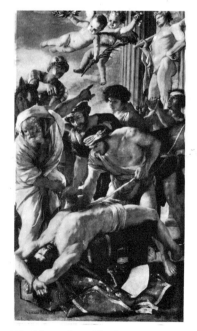

The Martyrdom of St. Erasmus
about 1629   *Rome, Vatican, Pin.*

The Eucharist, 1647
*Edinburgh, N. G. of Scotland, coll. Earl of Ellesmere*

favor of themes taken from classical history and legend. The figures in his compositions are carefully arranged to make plain the moral or narrative content, which Poussin considered extremely important, and are set in landscapes of appropriate solemnity. He often made small wax models to work out the construction of his pictures. In his later works the figures tended to be smaller, while the dominance of the landscape increased. In spite of his intellectual approach a poetic feeling for nature is apparent in his landscapes.

In 1640 Poussin reluctantly obeyed the repeated invitations of Louis XIII and Richelieu to go to Paris. As an official mission, the visit was a failure. He was forced to work hurriedly at uncongenial tasks, altarpieces, huge allegorical pictures, and decorations for the Louvre. He was hampered, moreover, by the jealous intrigues of established artists such as Simon Vouet, who felt their position threatened by his arrival. In 1642, on the pretext of fetching his wife, he returned thankfully to Rome, but the visit to Paris had not been entirely unprofitable. He had established contact with a group of friends in Paris who were to be his patrons for the rest of his life. For these men, pious, well-educated bourgeois of unostentatious but solid wealth, Poussin painted heroic and stoical subjects from Roman history and legend and dramatic Biblical scenes. These late works, in their geometrically exact composition, the stress laid upon their intellectual and moral content, and in the subordination of color to the unity of the whole represent the purest Classicism of French painting. Poussin's name was cited by those who followed him in these practices in their dispute with the Rubenists, who believed in the use of color as an aid to naturalism. Poussin dominated his own century and has exercised an important influence on French painting ever since.

Bacchanal
*London, N. G.*

## HIS WORKS INCLUDE

The Massacre of the Innocents
*Chantilly, Mus. Condé*
Parnassus
*Madrid, Prado*
The Israelites Gathering Manna
*Paris, Louvre*
Time Revealing Truth
*Paris, Louvre*
Landscape with a Snake, 1648
*London, N. G.*
Rest on the Flight into Egypt
*Leningrad, Hermitage*
Autumn
*Paris, Louvre*

**See also pages 104, 105, 106, 173, 174**

Selene and Endymion
*Detroit, Mich., Inst. of Arts*

The Adoration of the Golden Calf
(detail)
*London, N. G.*

73

## PIERRE PAUL PRUD'HON

*A quasi-classical artist of Romantic emotionalism*

Prud'hon was the most original of Jacques Louis David's contemporaries. As a boy of 16 he was sent by the Bishop of Mâcon from his home at Cluny to the Academy at Dijon, where he had his earliest training. From there he went to Paris, where he worked for engravers, and, in 1784, on to Rome on the proceeds of a prize. In Rome he did little work, but became a friend of the sculptor Antonio Canova. His own painting is not Neoclassical in style, but was strongly influenced by Leonardo and even more by Correggio.

On his return to Paris Prud'hon became the only rival of David and his pupils, finding success through the patronage of both Napoleon's empresses. He painted many portraits, mostly of women, elegant myths, and allegories such as *Justice and Vengeance Pursuing Crime*. A faulty technique has caused many of his portraits and paintings to deteriorate.

Venus and Adonis, 1810
*London, Wallace Coll.*

HIS WORKS INCLUDE

Portrait of Monsieur
Anthony, 1796
*Dijon, Mus. des B-A.*
Psyche, 1808
*Paris, Louvre*

**See also pages 140, 185**

Justice and Vengeance Pursuing Crime
(detail) 1808   *Paris, Louvre*

---

## PIERRE PUGET

*The most Baroque of the 17th-century French artists*

Pierre Puget was born in Marseilles in 1620. When he was 20 he went to Italy, where he lived for three years in Florence and Rome. His master was Pietro da Cortona, under whom Puget worked on the decorations of the Pitti Palace in Florence.

In 1643 Puget returned to Marseilles. He worked there and in Toulon, designing the decoration of warships and executing paintings for churches. In 1656 he was commissioned to work on the door of the Town Hall at Toulon. The two herms that support the lintel are in the Baroque manner; they show anguish and strain in every line of their expressions and posture.

In 1659 Puget came to the notice of Louis XIV's minister Nicolas Fouquet and was commissioned by him to do a resting Hercules. Puget selected his marble with

Alexander and Diogenes, 1671-93
*Paris, Louvre*

care, and settled in Genoa to work on the statue. But before he could finish it, political intrigue reversed his good fortune. Fouquet was disgraced and was succeeded by Jean Baptiste Colbert. From then on, Puget had little chance of success at court. It is probable that, apart from a basic lack of sympathy between the cold and circumspect minister and the arrogant, outspoken artist, Colbert rightly realized that any work of Puget's would strike a discordant note in Charles Lebrun's scheme for Versailles. Whatever the exact proportion of good sense and personal enmity in Colbert's attitude toward Puget, it is certain that Puget was given no important commissions and was not allowed anywhere near Versailles.

For a while Puget stayed in Genoa, and built up a substantial local reputation. His most important works there were two statues of St. Sebastian and one of the Blessed Alessandro Sauli, executed for the Sauli family.

In 1670 Puget found two blocks of marble abandoned in the docks at Toulon. With difficulty he got permission from Colbert's ministry to use them. From them he produced the statue *Milo of Crotona* and the relief *Alexander and Diogenes*, his greatest works. The *Milo* demonstrates once more Puget's power of showing the human body under strain. The statue was despatched to the king at Versailles in the care of Puget's son, and arrived there in 1683. After days of suspense the king approved it, and it was put in a prominent position. The encouragement stimulated Puget to further efforts, but his hopes were unfounded. Later works were refused by the king, and for those that were accepted the payment was often tardy and hard to get. To a certain extent, Puget's lack of success at court was inherent in his own nature, for he was a romantic artist, insisting on his own individuality in an age of tyranny and Classicism. Puget died in Marseilles in 1694.

Man Carrying a Sack of Grain,
about 1656
*London, V. and A.*

P PVGET

HIS WORKS INCLUDE

St. Sebastian (marble statue)
about 1665
*Genoa, S. Maria di Carignano*

St. Charles Borromeo, 1694
*Marseilles, Mus. Longchamp*

Hercules (marble)
*Paris, Louvre*

**See also page 201**

---

# ENGUERRAND QUARTON                    active 1447-1461

*One of the two greatest French painters of the 15th century*

Enguerrand Quarton was born in the diocese of Laon, probably about 1410. Little is known of his life. It is generally accepted, however, that he is the same person as Charanton and Charton; all three names are mentioned in documents between 1447 and 1461. He worked in Aix-en-Provence and in Avignon.

Two masterpieces are known to be his. In 1452 he collaborated with Pierre Villate on a *Madonna of Mercy*, and in 1454 he painted a *Coronation of the Virgin* at Villeneuve-les-Avignon. For the latter painting the contract still exists, and it dictates the subject matter in great detail.

Quarton's art was influenced both by the tradition of French monumental sculpture and by Gothic illumination. His works represent a perfect and extremely original synthesis, combining a decorative abstraction of form and a strong sense of reality. Quarton and Jean Fouquet were the greatest painters in 15th-century France. The Avignon *Pietà* is attributed to Quarton by some scholars.

SCHOOL OF AVIGNON
Attrib. to Enguerrand Quarton
Pietà (detail) mid 15th cent.
*Paris, Louvre*

HIS WORKS INCLUDE

The Madonna of Mercy, 1452
*Chantilly, Mus. Condé*

**See also page 86**

The Tomb of Philippe de Gueldres
Duchess of Lorraine, about 1550
*Nancy, Church of the Cordeliers*

## HIS WORKS INCLUDE

Head of Christ, about 1554
*Paris, Société de l'Histoire de Protestantisme*

The Easter Sepulchre
*Saint Mihiel, Church of St. Étienne*

**See also page 196**

# LIGIER RICHIER          about 1500-1566/7

*A sculptor who spent much of his life in the service of the dukes of Lorraine*

Richier was born in St. Mihiel in Lorraine. There are not many statues that can be attributed to him with certainty, but his style appears to have been typical of much contemporary French sculpture, with a mixture of Gothic naturalism and Italian influence in his treatment of draperies. This is particularly true of the Easter Sepulchre in the Church of St. Étienne in Saint Mihiel.

For the tomb of Philippe de Gueldres, Duchess of Lorraine, who died in 1547, Richier sculptured a recumbent effigy in which the face is treated with a particularly northern type of naturalism. This tomb is in the church of the Cordeliers at Nancy. In the Church of St. Pierre at Bar-le-Duc there is figure of a skeleton on the tomb of René de Châlons that is attributed to Richier, although there is no documentary evidence to prove this. His obsession with skeletons is typical of the late Gothic period. Richier himself was caught up in the religious unrest of the time, and was converted to Protestantism. Eventually he fled to Geneva, where he died in 1566 or 1567.

---

Self-portrait
*Florence, Uffizi*

*H·Rig.*

## HIS WORKS INCLUDE

Portrait of Marie Cadenne, 1684
*Caen, Mus. des B-A.*

Portrait of Philippe V, 1700
*Paris, Louvre*

Portrait of Louis XIV, 1701
*Paris, Louvre*

Portrait of Jacques Bénigne Bossuet, 1702
*Paris, Louvre*

**See also page 116**

# HYACINTHE RIGAUD          1659-1743

*A prolific portrait painter with several styles*

Hyacinthe Rigaud was born in Perpignan near the Spanish border. When he was 15 he went to Montpellier and thence to Lyons, studying under various masters. By 1681 he had reached Paris, where he spent some years painting portraits of other artists and members of the bourgeoisie, which are usually held to be his best works.

In 1688 Rigaud's professional life suddenly changed; he was commissioned to paint the king's brother, and in the following year he painted the brother's son. After this he became almost exclusively a court painter, and his clientele consisted of royalty, generals, visiting princes, and diplomats. His portraits were usually in the elegant manner of van Dyck, but the inventory taken of Rigaud's goods when he married in 1703 includes seven of Rembrandt's paintings and two copies of his work. So Rembrandt, at that time almost ignored in France, was evidently a favorite with Rigaud, and this influence is to be seen in his less formal portraits of his family and friends. The naturalism of these works, for example the double portrait of his mother, is in strong contrast to such works as the Baroque full-length state portrait of Louis XIV with its billowing ermine and elegantly placed feet.

Rigaud was a most prolific and prosperous painter. With the help of his pupils and assistants he produced an average of 35 portraits a year for 62 years, before his death at the advanced age of 84. His style of court portrait became the accepted one throughout Europe during the 18th century.

# HUBERT ROBERT

1733-1808

*A painter of architectural fantasies and landscapes*

Hubert Robert's father was the valet of the Marquis de Stainville, whose son was French Ambassador to the Holy See. Through his patronage, Robert entered the French Academy in Rome and enrolled as a student of Giovanni Paolo Panini, an Italian painter of picturesque ruins. Robert became friendly with his master and also with Giovanni Battista Piranesi, who etched Roman antiquities in a strongly poetic manner. From these friends Robert derived his style, calculated to bring out the picturesque and romantic qualities of ruins and old buildings. Poetry, not accuracy, was his intention.

In 1761 Robert traveled in southern Italy with Jean Honoré Fragonard. On his return to Paris in 1765 he became a member of the Academy, and found his work greatly in demand. He did some decorative compositions for various great houses and painted Parisian views and street scenes. He was one of the first curators of the Louvre. In 1783 Robert visited the south of France to paint the Roman remains there; the Maison Carrée at Nîmes and the Pont du Gard. On the outbreak of the Revolution in 1789 Robert painted scenes of violence and unrest in Paris. He spent some time in prison himself, but continued to paint. He was released when Robespierre fell from power, and made one more trip to Italy before 1802.

## HIS WORKS INCLUDE

A Fountain under a Portico
*Paris, Louvre*
The Curved Staircase
*Paris, Louvre*
View of the Capitol
*Valenciennes, Mus. des B-A.*
View of a Park, about 1783
*Paris, Louvre*

**See also pages 136, 184**

The Port of Ripetta
*Paris, École des B-A.*

Cascades of Tivoli
*Paris, Louvre*

Rocks
*London, N. G.*

**TH. Rousseau**

HIS WORKS INCLUDE

The Descent of the Cows, about 1833
*Amiens, Mus. de Picardie*

Avenue of Chestnut Trees, 1834
*Paris, Louvre*

View of the Plain of Montmartre,
about 1848
*Paris, Louvre*

View of the Landes, 1852
*Paris, Louvre*

River Scene
*London, N. G.*

**See also page 158**

# THÉODORE ROUSSEAU 1812-1867

*A painter of landscapes*

Théodore Rousseau was born in Paris on April 15, 1812, the son of a tailor. Precociously gifted, he never went to Italy to study, but worked in the French countryside, modeling his work on the naturalistic landscape painting of the Dutch masters. He also admired the English painter Constable, whose *Hay-Wain* he saw in 1833. He made his Salon debut in 1831 with a *Landscape of Auvergne*, but was so consistently refused from 1836 until 1848 that he became known as "le grand Refusé."

In 1844 Rousseau settled at Barbizon on the edge of the Fontainebleau Forest, which he had visited several times before. He was later joined by his friends Jean François Millet and Diaz de la Peña, and the group became known as the Barbizon school.

In the 1855 Paris Universal Exhibition, Rousseau showed many paintings, but he never gained many patrons or became widely known. After an unsuccessful auction of some of his works in 1861 he contemplated leaving France, but was unable to do this because his wife was almost insane and his father dependent on him. In 1863 he traveled to the Alps and made sketches of Mont Blanc, but he fell ill and returned to Barbizon, where he died four years later.

Rousseau's paintings of the forest are simple in composition and display great attention to detail, intense local color and sometimes a symbolic element in his choice of subjects. The inherent romanticism of his approach to nature becomes clear when his landscapes are compared with those of the Impressionists.

The Forest at Fontainebleau, about 1848
*Paris, Louvre*

The Banks of the Loire, about 1855
*Paris, Louvre*

# FRANÇOIS RUDE                           1784-1855

*An ardent supporter of Napoleon*

François Rude was born in Dijon in 1784, and later went to Paris to study at the École des Beaux-Arts. He was an ardent supporter of Napoleon, and he was forced to flee to Brussels after the Emperor's downfall in 1814. He did not return to France until 1827.

During 1835 and 1836 Rude was working on *The Departure of the Volunteers in 1792* for the Arc de Triomphe in Paris. This dramatic relief shows some similarity to Delacroix's painting of *Liberty Guiding the People*, exhibited at the Salon in 1831, and has an analogy with the vigorous style of Pierre Puget's sculpture. The relief, which is generally referred to as *The Marseillaise*, contains several conventional details but is forceful in its impact on the spectator.

The bronze *Awakening of Napoleon*, on which Rude worked from 1845 to 1847, shows a skillful use of shadow to give a heightened sense of form. A strong sculptural element and a vivacity of detail make the statue of the mathematician Gaspard Monge and the monument to Marshal Ney in Paris outstanding among the works being produced at that time in France. Jean Baptiste Carpeaux was influenced by Rude; he made a crayon drawing of the head of "Revolution" from *The Marseillaise*, and modeled his *Fisher-boy with a Shell* of 1855 to 1859 on a sculpture by Rude.

Joan of Arc
*Paris, Louvre*

HIS WORKS INCLUDE

Theseus (bronze) from 1806
*Paris, Louvre*

Maréchal de Saxe, about 1835
*Versailles, Château*

Imperial Eagle Watching Over the Dead Napoleon (bronze) about 1845
*Paris, Louvre*

The Virgin and St. John
(bronze) 1848-52
*Paris, St. Vincent-de-Paul*

Maréchal Ney, 1852-53
*Paris, Place Camille Julian*

**See also page 209**

The Marseillaise (detail) 1836
*Paris, Arc de Triomphe*

---

# GABRIEL JACQUES DE ST. AUBIN          1724-1780

*A painter, draftsman, and engraver of 18th-century Parisian life*

Gabriel Jacques de St. Aubin spent his entire life in Paris. His brothers Charles and Augustin were also artists and engravers, and the three brothers all had successful careers. Gabriel de St. Aubin studied under Étienne Jeaurat at the Academy, and was also the pupil of François Boucher. It is known that he tried unsuccessfully for the Prix de Rome. Although he produced some pleasant paintings in oil he was best known for his drawings and engravings which are among the most accomplished in the 18th century. He died in 1780, leaving an exhaustive record of contemporary life in Paris, in a series of engravings which even today, like the greater part of his oeuvre, are not yet known to the general public.

HIS WORKS INCLUDE

Meeting on the Boulevard,
about 1760
*Perpignan, Mus. des B-A.*

A Street Show
*London, N. G.*

Dream of Voltaire, about 1778
*Paris, Louvre*

Sketch Books
*Paris, Bibl. Nat., et al.*

**See also page 181**

Two Children with a Goat
*Paris, Louvre*

HIS WORKS INCLUDE

Altar, about 1627
*Paris, St. Roch*
Monument of Cardinal de Bérulle
*Paris, Louvre*

**See also page 199**

# JACQUES SARRAZIN 1588/92-1660

*The dominant sculptor of the mid-17th century*

Born in Noyon near Compiègne, Jacques Sarrazin received his first training from a sculptor, Nicolas Guillain. Between 1610 and about 1626 he lived in Rome, where he came under the influence of various classical artists.

Sarrazin's mature style appears in his first royal commission, the decoration of the Pavillon de l'Horloge at the Louvre. This is the earliest example of French Classicism in sculpture. From 1642 to 1650 Sarrazin designed the decorations for the Château of Maisons-Lafitte for the architect François Mansart, but the actual work was carried out by his pupils.

Sarrazin's last great work was the sculpture for a tomb for Henry of Bourbon. This was begun in 1648, but the civil unrest of the first and second Fronde interrupted the work and the tomb was not completed until after his death. In the 19th century it was moved from its original site in the Church of St. Paul and St. Louis in Paris to Chantilly, so Sarrazin's intentions for the grouping can only be conjectured. The separate groups are free in their movement and the drapery is amply folded in the Baroque manner. They would not look out of place at Versailles, and in fact a *Sphinx and Children* was carried out from Sarrazin's designs after his death for the gardens there. Sarrazin's style dominated the middle of the 17th century, and all the young sculptors of the next generation were his pupils.

St. Louis Giving Alms to the Poor
(detail)
*Versailles, Château*

# MICHEL ANGE SLODTZ 1705-1764

*A Baroque sculptor and decorator*

René Michel Slodtz, called "Michel Ange," was born in Paris on September 27, 1705, the youngest son of a family of sculptors. He became his father's pupil, and later attended the Academy school, where he won the second prize for sculpture in 1724 and 1726. Two years later he was awarded a grant to go to the French Academy in Rome. He remained in Rome until 1747, although he had left the Academy in 1736, and had probably revisited France in 1743. During his stay in Rome Slodtz made a statue of *St. Bruno* for St. Peter's and copied Michelangelo's *Risen Christ* in the Church of Santa Maria sopra Minerva. He also made the tomb of the Marquis Caponi, and the mausoleum for the Archbishop Montmorin and the Archbishop de La Tour d'Auvergne, which was executed between 1740 and 1744.

When Slodtz returned to Paris he was made an associate of the Academy. At the end of 1749 he collaborated with his brothers and was concerned with the decorations for the celebration of the birth of the Duke of Burgundy. Later he designed the catafalques for the funeral decorations for the Spanish king in Notre Dame.

Slodtz also worked in many churches. In St. Sulpice he sculpted his masterpiece, the tomb of the Curé Languet de Gergy, and made decorations for the porch. He worked at Fontainebleau and in the Cathedral of Bourges, in Notre

Dame, and in the Château and Chapel of Choisy. He also decorated some buildings in the Place Louis XV (now known as the Place de la Concorde). The general character of his work is essentially Baroque in feeling.

In 1755 Slodtz was given a pension, which was later increased, and a year afterwards he was made an associate of the Academy of Sciences, Belles-Lettres, and Arts at Rouen. He died in Paris of a chest disease in October, 1764.

HIS WORKS INCLUDE

Bust of Nicolas Vleughels,
*Paris, Mus. Jacquemart-André*
St. Bruno
*Rome, St. Peter's*
Tomb of Archbishop Montmorin,
about 1747
*Vienne, Cath.*

**See also page 206**

---

# JEAN FRANÇOIS DE TROY                    1679-1752

*A painter of Rococo decorative compositions*

Jean François de Troy was born in Paris, where his father was a portrait painter. He spent six years of his youth in Rome. Gifted with great facility in different genres, he soon became a fashionable painter, working in the Rococo style.

In 1738 de Troy became the director of the French Academy in Rome. During his period of office there was a great deal of trouble over the quality of the work sent to France from Rome by the state-subsidized pupils of the Academy. De Troy defended his pupils, but the trouble lay with the defective training received in Paris. For this reason the École des Élèves Protégés was founded in 1748 to give a chosen dozen students a better groundwork in education so that they could profit more from their three years in Rome. His relations with the administration in Paris were always difficult after this. As a result, when he asked for his recall his request was accepted ungraciously if not rudely. In his last few weeks as director, he fell in love with a young and beautiful Roman girl, and his grief and despair at having to go led to a fever from which he died in 1752.

De Troy's work was both varied and abundant, comprising allegorical and decorative compositions, portraits and historical pictures.

Self-portrait
*Florence, Uffizi*

Henry IV with Fellow Members of
the Order of the Saint-Esprit, 1732
*Paris, Mus. de la Légion d'Honneur*

A Hunt Breakfast, 1737
*London, Wallace Coll.*

**I DETROY**

HIS WORKS INCLUDE

The Alarm, 1723
*London, V. and A.*
Death of a Stag, 1737
*London, Wallace Coll.*
The Swooning of Esther, 1737
*Paris, Louvre*

**See also page 117**

The Cheat
*Dresden, Gemäldegal.*

HIS WORKS INCLUDE

Judith
*Toulouse, Mus. des Augustins*
The Concert
*Paris, Louvre*
The Judgment of Solomon
*Paris, Louvre*

**See also page 98**

## LE VALENTIN

1594-1632

*A French Caravaggesque painter*

Born at Coulommiers, near Paris, Le Valentin, otherwise known as Moïse Valentin, or Valentin de Boullogne, was in Rome by 1614 at the latest. There he was probably on friendly terms with Simon Vouet. He was much influenced by Bartolommeo Manfredi. Of all French artists who followed Caravaggio, Valentin did so the most closely. He shed all his French characteristics, painting full-blooded pictures of military life, card sharpers, and fortune tellers. He achieved great technical virtuosity.

Valentin painted a pendant to Poussin's altarpiece *The Martyrdom of St. Erasmus* called *The Martyrdom of Saints Processus and Martinian* for St. Peter's, Rome. This, his only documented work, was painted about 1630. His paintings were admired by Louis XIV, who owned some of them, and he was also patronized by Pope Urban VIII. Although many of his pictures were sent to France, where they were much in demand, Valentin lived and worked in Rome for the rest of his life.

*M. Valentin.*

---

Self-portrait
*Arles, Mus. des B-A.*

HIS WORKS INCLUDE

Wealth, formerly part of the
decoration of Château Neuf,
about 1630
*Paris, Louvre*
Lot and his Daughters, 1633
*Strasbourg, Mus. des B-A.*
Decoration for the Nymphaeum
*Wideville, France*

**See also pages 97, 170**

## SIMON VOUET

1590-1649

*An influential painter of religious and decorative works*

Simon Vouet is said to have left home for England at the age of 14 to paint the portrait of a French lady living there. Whether this is true or not, it is certain that in 1611 he traveled to Constantinople with a French ambassador. In 1613 he arrived in Venice. In 1614 he went to Rome; here his work showed the influence first of Caravaggio and later of a modified Baroque.

On his return to Paris in 1627, Vouet enjoyed immediate success as a painter of religious and mythogical subjects, under the patronage of Louis XIII and Cardinal Richelieu. In the sphere of decorative painting he followed Annibale Carracci in the illusion of reality given by the use of deep perspective and false architectural details. He held his position as the most important painter in Paris until his death, challenged only by the visit of Poussin in 1640.

Vouet was a versatile artist, but perhaps a rather superficial one. His value lies in the fact that he brought the stimulus of a new Italian idiom to French painting at a time when it was at a low ebb, and that he established a school of a Baroque movement. The clarity and decorative qualities of his work attracted the interest of his pupils Eustache Le Sueur and Charles Lebrun. The movement he instigated was halted about 1645 by the Classicism of Poussin and his followers.

## JEAN WARIN                                    1604-1672

*A sculptor and medallist*

Jean Warin produced many excellent portrait busts of eminent contemporaries. His style reflected the varied trends of the classical, naturalistic, and Baroque. Although Warin seems not to have visited Italy, he appears to have known some of the work of Bernini and of Alessandro Algardi. His work also continued the traditions of Germain Pilon. He was a more subtle artist than many of his contemporaries.

In 1629 Warin succeeded René Olivier in a position of importance in the French Mint, and later married his widow. Warin was continually at variance with his collaborator, Pierre Regnier. In 1646, after the death of Abraham Dupré, he was appointed head of the Mint, which he completely reorganized. Warin was admitted in 1665 as a member of the Academy, whose seal he had engraved in 1630. He was certainly the most brilliant medallist of the 17th century.

Louis XIII
*Paris, Louvre*

**See also page 200**

---

## ANTOINE WATTEAU                                1684-1721

*An artist who captured the exquisite frivolities of the 18th century*

Antoine Watteau's father was a tiler and carpenter in Valenciennes. A severe man, he was at first determined that his son should follow his trade, but he eventually capitulated and allowed Watteau to work with a hack painter in the town. Seeing that this was of little use to him, Watteau ran away to Paris in 1702 and found a job at the Pont-Notre-Dame producing endless copies of religious paintings. He said of this work "I knew my St. Nicolas by heart and had no need of the originals." He spent the little free time he had in drawing from nature.

It was probably during this time of hardship that Watteau contracted the tuberculosis that was to aggravate the natural restlessness of his temperament and to cause his early death. Fortunately, in about 1704, he met Claude Gillot, a painter of theatrical scenes. An affinity of taste, character, and temperament soon led to a close friendship, but when Watteau began to outshine his master the two parted company on bad terms. Watteau never tried to deny the debt that he owed

FRANÇOIS BOUCHER
Portrait of Antoine Watteau
*Chantilly, Mus. Condé*

The Music Lesson (detail) about 1717
*London, Wallace Coll.*

"La Gamme d'Amour" (detail)
*London, N. G.*

## HIS WORKS INCLUDE

Portrait of Antoine Pater
*Valenciennes, Mus. des B-A.*

A Halt during the Chase
*London, Wallace Coll.*

Jupiter and Antiope
*Paris, Louvre*

Venetian Festival
*Edinburgh, N. G. of Scotland*

Italian Comedians
*Washington, D. C., N. G.*

The Judgment of Paris
*Paris, Louvre*

Recreations of War
*Leningrad, Hermitage*

**See also pages 118, 119, 120, 179, 180**

Gillot; Gillot abandoned painting and devoted himself to etching and engraving.

By 1707 Watteau had joined the decorative painter Claude Audran, who was the steward of the Luxembourg Palace. This meant that Watteau was able to study and copy Rubens' paintings there. The informal beauty of the Luxembourg Gardens, bathed in a golden evening light, forms the backcloth for the elegant creatures of his paintings who meet for conversation or dalliance. It was Watteau's practice to fill a sketchbook with quick figure drawings and to use them in his canvases as he wanted them.

Watteau gained second place in the competition for the Prix de Rome, and after a short return visit to Valenciennes he became in 1712 an associate of the Academy. He should then have submitted a diploma work, but he delayed this until 1717, when, on the strength of his painting *The Embarkation for Cythera*, he was admitted to full membership as a painter of *fêtes galantes*, the first to be so described.

Success brought Watteau no real happiness. His young friend the Comte de Caylus speaks of "the very ephemeral nature of all satisfactions for a man of Watteau's temper." His election to the Academy brought him all the distracting attentions of polite society and the annoyance of predatory dealers making off with sketches or discarded canvases. Little or none of this frustration and unhappiness shows in his work, which seems to realize a perfect world of sunlit calm shared with delightful company.

Watteau lived with various of his friends, finding it hard to settle in any one place for long. In 1720 his always poor health deteriorated, and on the dubious advice of a chance acquaintance he took a trip to London to consult a certain Dr. Mead. He soon returned to Paris to stay with his friend Edmé François Gersaint, the picture dealer, for whom "to loosen up his fingers" he painted a shop sign. This work, completed in an amazingly short time considering Watteau's failing strength, shows in its telling postures and carefully rendered textures the beginnings of a new naturalism. But no new development of his genius was to be allowed him; he wanted to return to Valenciennes, but his strength was not equal to the journey. He died on July 18, 1721.

The Music Party (detail)
*London, Wallace Coll.*

Recruits Rejoining the Regiment
*Paris, Bibl. Nat.*

POL, HENNEQUIN, and HERMANN DE LIMBOURG
April, from the *Très Riches Heures du Duc de Berri*, begun 1415 *vellum* 8¼ × 5¼ *in.*
*Chantilly, Musée Condé*

ENGUERRAND QUARTON   The Coronation of the Virgin, 1454   *oil on panel*   *72 × 86⅝ in.*
*Villeneuve-les-Avignon, Hospice*

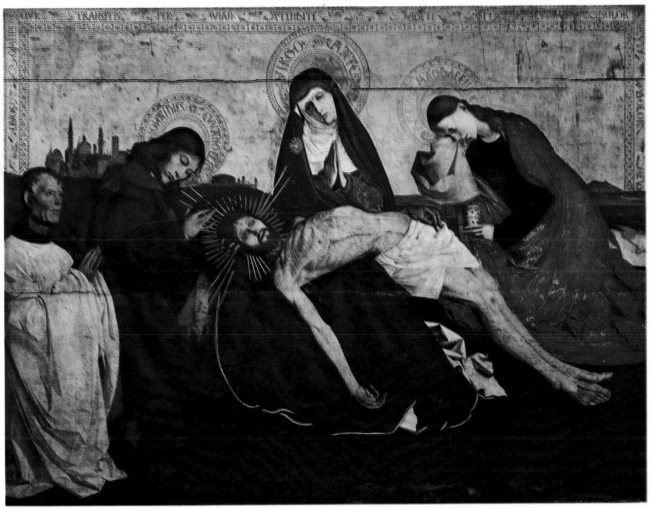

SCHOOL OF AVIGNON (Attributed to Enguerrand Quarton)  Pietà, mid 15th century  *oil on panel  63¾ × 85⅞ in.*
*Paris, Louvre*

HENRI BELLECHOSE    The Communion and Martyrdom of St. Denis, about 1416    *oil on panel    63¾ × 82⅝ in.*
*Paris, Louvre*

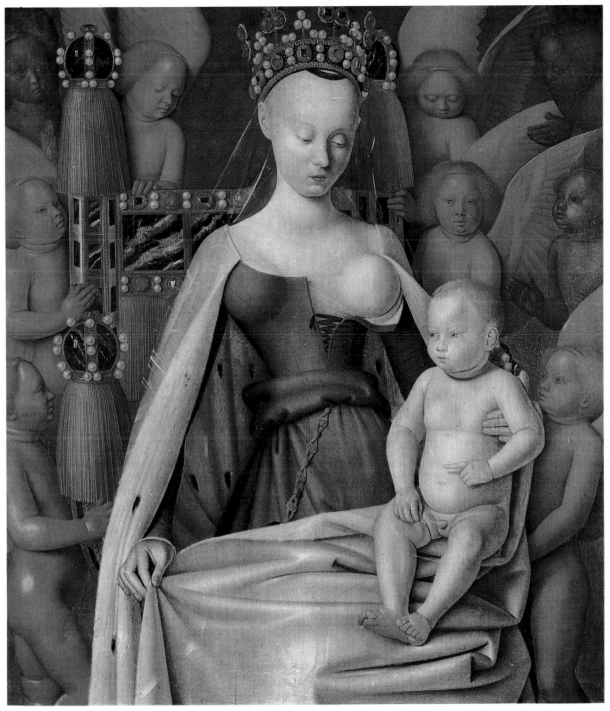

JEAN FOUQUET  The Madonna and Child with Angels, about 1450  *oil on panel*  $37\frac{3}{8} \times 33\frac{7}{8}$ *in.*
*Antwerp, Musée Royal des Beaux-Arts*

JEAN FOUQUET   Étienne Chevalier with St. Stephen, about 1450   *oil on panel*   *36⅝ × 33¼ in.*
*West Berlin, Staatliche Museen*

MASTER OF THE AIX ANNUNCIATION  The Aix Annunciation, about 1444  *oil on panel  61 × 69¼ in.*
*Aix-en-Provence, Church of La Madeleine*

SIMON MARMION   The Life of St. Bertin, about 1459   *oil on panel*   *22 × 52¼ in.*
*West Berlin, Staatliche Museen*

NICOLAS FROMENT   The Virgin in the Burning Bush, 1476
*oil on panel   162 × 118 in.*
*Aix-en-Provence, Cathedral*

MASTER OF MOULINS  The Madonna and Child with Angels (detail) about 1498  *oil on panel*
*Moulins, Cathedral*

94

FRANÇOIS CLOUET  Pierre Quthe, 1562  *oil on panel  $37\frac{7}{8} \times 27\frac{1}{8}$ in.*
*Paris, Louvre*

SCHOOL OF FONTAINEBLEAU (Attributed to François Clouet)    The Bath of Diana, about 1550-60    *oil on canvas*    52⅜×75⅝ *in.*
*Rouen, Musée des Beaux-Arts*

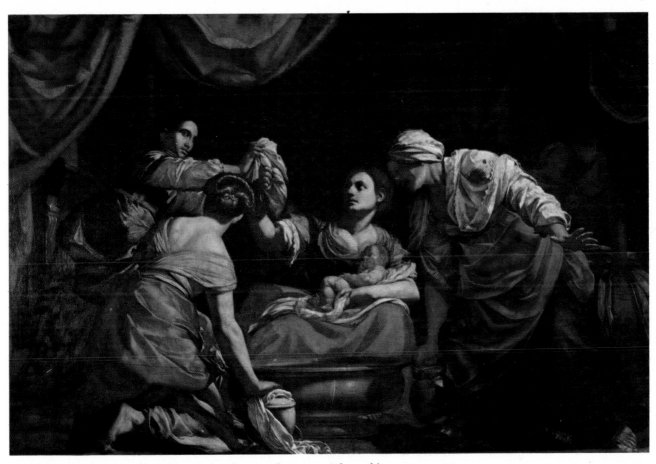

SIMON VOUET  The Birth of the Virgin, 1615-20  *oil on canvas  85½ × 129½ in.*
*Rome, S. Francesco a Ripa*

LE VALENTIN  The Four Ages of Man    *oil on canvas*   *38 × 52¾ in.*
*London, National Gallery*

LOUIS LE NAIN  The Peasants' Meal, 1642  *oil on canvas  38¼ × 48 in.*
*Paris, Louvre*

LOUIS LE NAIN  Landscape with Figures, about 1643   *oil on canvas*   *21½ × 26¼ in.*
*London, Victoria and Albert Museum*

MATHIEU LE NAIN   The Backgammon Players, about 1650   *oil on canvas*   $35\frac{3}{8} \times 47\frac{1}{4}$ *in.*
*Paris, Louvre*

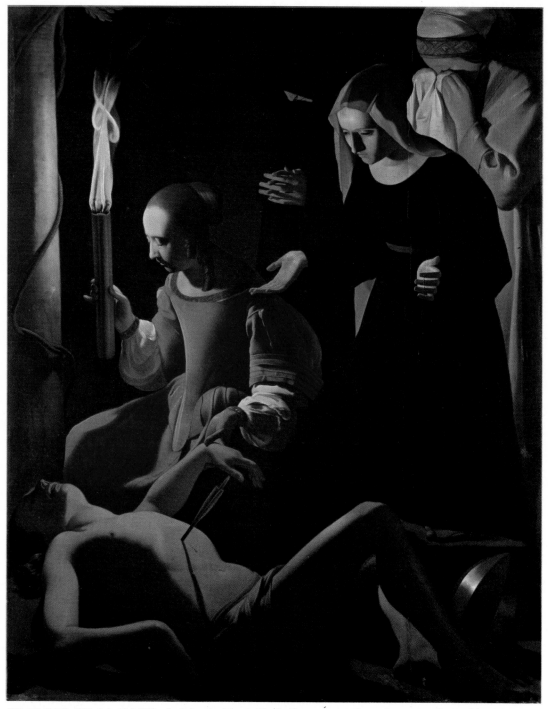

GEORGES DE LA TOUR   St. Sebastian Tended by St. Irene, about 1630   *oil on canvas   63 × 50¾ in.*
*West Berlin, Staatliche Museen*

GEORGES DE LA TOUR  The Newborn Child  *oil on canvas*  $29\frac{7}{8} \times 35\frac{7}{8}$ *in.*
*Rennes, Musée de Rennes*

NICOLAS POUSSIN  The Inspiration of the Poet, 1629   *oil on canvas   72½ × 84¼ in.*
*Paris, Louvre*

**NICOLAS POUSSIN** Diogenes, 1648 *oil on canvas 63 × 87 in.*
*Paris, Louvre*

NICOLAS POUSSIN  Apollo and Daphne, about 1665  *oil on canvas  61 × 102¼ in.*
*Paris, Louvre*

JACQUES BLANCHARD  Charity, 1637  *oil on canvas*  $41\frac{1}{2} \times 31\frac{3}{4}$ *in.*
*London, Courtauld Institute Galleries*

CLAUDE GELLÉE LORRAINE   The Embarkation of the Queen of Sheba, 1648   *oil on canvas   58¼ × 76¼ in.*
*London, National Gallery*

CLAUDE GELLÉE LORRAINE  Europa, 1667  *oil on canvas  40×53 in.*
*London, Royal Collection*

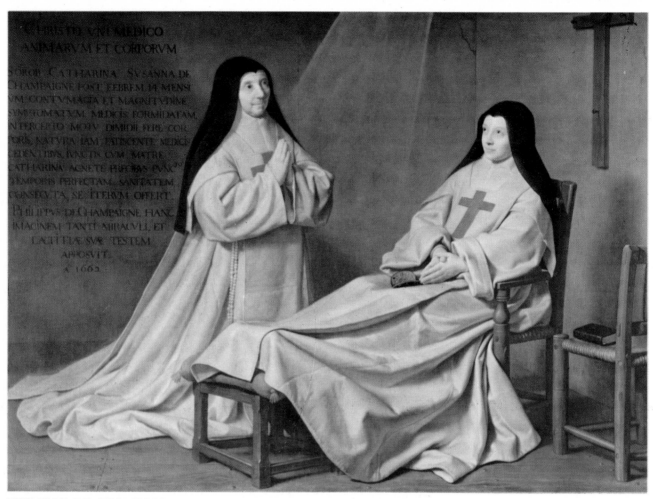

PHILIPPE DE CHAMPAIGNE  Two Nuns of Port Royal, 1662   *oil on canvas*   *65 × 90¼ in.*
*Paris, Louvre*

**SÉBASTIEN BOURDON**  L'Homme aux Rubans Noirs, 1655-60  *oil on canvas*  *41¾ × 33½ in.*
*Montpellier, Musée Fabre*

EUSTACHE LE SUEUR  The Mass of St. Martin, about 1655  *oil on canvas*  *44⅜ × 33¼ in.*
*Paris, Louvre*

**BAUGIN**   The Five Senses   *oil on panel   21¾ × 28¾ in.*
*Paris, Louvre*

CHARLES LEBRUN  Chancellor Séguier, about 1660  *oil on canvas*  *116 × 137¾ in.*
*Paris, Louvre*

NICOLAS DE LARGILLIERRE  The Artist and his Family  *oil on canvas  $58\frac{3}{4} \times 78\frac{3}{4}$ in.*
*Paris, Louvre*

HYACINTHE RIGAUD  The Artist's Mother, 1695   *oil on canvas   31⅞ × 39¾ in.*
*Paris, Louvre*

JEAN FRANÇOIS DE TROY  Le Déjeuner d'Huitres, 1734  *oil on canvas  70¾ × 49¾ in.*
*Chantilly, Musée Condé*

ANTOINE WATTEAU   The Embarkation for Cythera, 1717   *oil on canvas   $50\frac{3}{4} \times 76\frac{1}{4}$ in.*
*Paris, Louvre*

ANTOINE WATTEAU   The Signboard for the Shop of the Art Dealer Gersaint, 1720   *oil on canvas*   $54\frac{1}{4} \times 121\frac{1}{4}$ *in.*
*West Berlin, Staatliche Museen*

ANTOINE WATTEAU  Gilles, 1721  *oil on canvas*  $72\frac{1}{2} \times 58\frac{5}{8}$ *in.*
*Paris, Louvre*

JEAN BAPTISTE OUDRY  The Dead Wolf, 1721  *oil on canvas  75 × 100½ in.*
*London, Wallace Collection*

NICOLAS LANCRET   Italian Comedians by a Fountain, about 1720   *oil on canvas   36 × 33 in.*
*London, Wallace Collection*

**JEAN BAPTISTE JOSEPH PATER**  The Dance  *oil on canvas*  *22¼ × 18 in.*
*London, Wallace Collection*

JEAN BAPTISTE SIMÉON CHARDIN  The Skate, 1728  *oil on canvas*  44⅞ × 57½ *in.*
*Paris, Louvre*

JEAN BAPTISTE SIMÉON CHARDIN  Le Bénédicité, about 1740  *oil on canvas*  *19¼ × 15 in.*
*Paris, Louvre*

JEAN BAPTISTE SIMÉON CHARDIN Self-portrait, 1775  *pastel*  *18⅛ × 15 in.*
*Paris, Louvre*

FRANÇOIS BOUCHER   The Toilet of Venus, 1746   *oil on canvas*   $38\frac{5}{8} \times 51\frac{3}{8}$ in.
*Stockholm, Nationalmuseum*

FRANÇOIS BOUCHER  Madame de Pompadour, about 1757  *oil on canvas*  13¾ × 17¼ *in.*
*Edinburgh, National Gallery of Scotland*

MAURICE QUENTIN DE LATOUR  Self-portrait, 1751  *pastel*  $25\frac{1}{4} \times 20\frac{7}{8}$ *in.*
*Amiens, Musée de Picardie*

JEAN MARC NATTIER  Marie Lecsinska, 1762  *oil on canvas*  *76¼ × 57 in.*
*Warsaw, National Museum*

JEAN BAPTISTE PERRONNEAU  Madame de Sorquainville, 1749  *oil on canvas*  $39\frac{3}{8} \times 31\frac{1}{2}$ *in.*
*Paris, Louvre*

JOSEPH SIFFREIN DUPLESSIS   Gluck at the Clavichord, 1775   *oil on canvas   39 × 31½ in.*
*Vienna, Kunsthistorisches Museum*

**JEAN BAPTISTE GREUZE** Mademoiselle Sophie Arnould, about 1769 *oil on canvas 24 × 20 in.*
*London, Wallace Collection*

**JEAN HONORÉ FRAGONARD** The Swing, about 1766 *oil on canvas* 32⅛ × 26 *in.*
*London, Wallace Collection*

JEAN HONORÉ FRAGONARD   Fête of St. Cloud, about 1770   *oil on canvas*   *85 × 132¼ in.*
*Paris, Banque de France*

HUBERT ROBERT  Le Pont du Gard, 1787  *oil on canvas*  *95¼×95¼ in.*
*Paris, Louvre*

JACQUES LOUIS DAVID  The Oath of the Horatii, 1784   *oil on canvas   130 × 160 in.*
*Paris, Louvre*

JACQUES LOUIS DAVID  Madame Sériziat and her Child, about 1769  *oil on canvas*  $51\frac{1}{2} \times 37\frac{3}{4}$ *in.*
*Paris, Louvre*

JACQUES LOUIS DAVID  The Coronation of Napoleon and Josephine in Notre Dame (detail)
about 1807  *oil on canvas*  *240 × 366¼ in.*
*Paris, Louvre*

PIERRE PAUL PRUD'HON   Empress Josephine, 1805   *oil on canvas*   *96×70½ in.*
*Paris, Louvre*

FRANÇOIS GÉRARD  Isabey and his Daughter, 1795  *oil on canvas  $76\frac{3}{8} \times 49\frac{1}{4}$ in.*
*Paris, Louvre*

ANTOINE JEAN GROS  The Pesthouse at Jaffa, 1804  *oil on canvas  209½ × 283¾ in.*
*Paris, Louvre*

ANTOINE JEAN GROS  Napoleon at Arcola (detail) 1796  *oil on canvas*  $28\frac{3}{4} \times 23\frac{1}{4}$ *in.*
*Paris, Louvre*

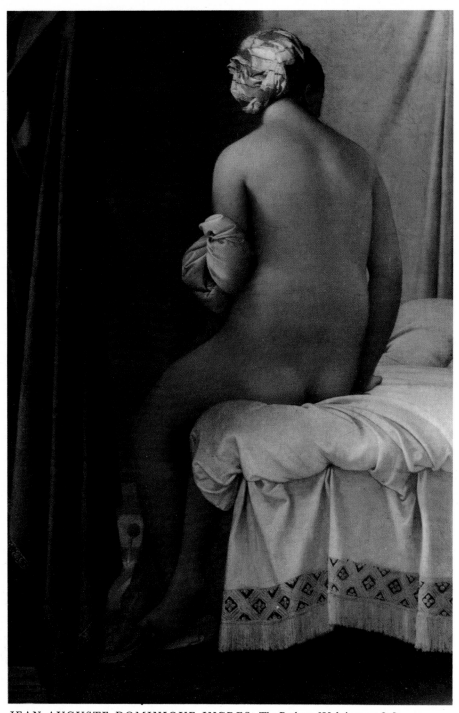

JEAN AUGUSTE DOMINIQUE INGRES  The Bather of Valpinçon, 1808
*oil on canvas  56¼ × 38¼ in.*
*Paris, Louvre*

JEAN AUGUSTE DOMINIQUE INGRES  Stratonice, 1840  *oil on canvas*  $22\frac{1}{2} \times 38\frac{1}{8}$ *in.*
*Chantilly, Musée Condé*

JEAN AUGUSTE DOMINIQUE INGRES  Madame Rivière, 1805  *oil on canvas*  $45\frac{5}{8} \times 38\frac{3}{8}$ *in.*
*Paris, Louvre*

THÉODORE GÉRICAULT  The Raft of the Medusa, 1819  *oil on canvas*  *193¼ × 281½ in.*
*Paris, Louvre*

THÉODORE GÉRICAULT  La Folle d'Envie, about 1824  *oil on canvas*  $28\frac{3}{8} \times 22\frac{5}{8}$ *in.*
*Lyons, Musée des Beaux-Arts*

THÉODORE GÉRICAULT  Epsom Racecourse, 1821   *oil on canvas*   $34\frac{5}{8} \times 47\frac{1}{4}$ *in.*
*Paris, Louvre*

JEAN BAPTISTE CAMILLE COROT  The Forum from the Farnese Gardens, 1826  *oil on canvas*  *11 × 19⅝ in.*
*Paris, Louvre*

JEAN BAPTISTE CAMILLE COROT  The Bridge at Narni, about 1827  *oil on canvas  14⅜ × 18½ in.*
*Paris, Louvre*

JEAN BAPTISTE CAMILLE COROT  Woman in Blue, 1874
*oil on canvas  31½ × 19⅝ in.*
*Paris, Louvre*

EUGÈNE DELACROIX  The Massacre at Chios, 1824  *oil on canvas  166 × 138½ in.*
*Paris, Louvre*

EUGÈNE DELACROIX  Liberty Guiding the People, 1830  *oil on canvas  102⅜ × 128 in.*
*Paris, Louvre*

EUGÈNE DELACROIX  Women of Algiers, 1834  *oil on canvas*  $69\frac{5}{8} \times 89\frac{3}{4}$ *in.*
*Paris, Louvre*

HONORÉ DAUMIER  Don Quixote, about 1865  *oil on canvas*  *39½ × 32 in.*
*London, Courtauld Institute Galleries*

JEAN FRANÇOIS MILLET   The Gleaners, 1857   *oil on canvas*   $33\frac{1}{8} \times 43\frac{3}{4}$ *in.*
*Paris, Louvre*

THÉODORE ROUSSEAU  Spring, about 1852  *oil on canvas  16⅜ × 25 in.*
*Paris, Louvre*

THÉODORE CHASSÉRIAU   The Two Sisters, 1843   *oil on canvas   70⅝ × 53 in.*
*Paris, Louvre*

GUSTAVE COURBET   Portrait of the Artist with a Black Dog, 1842   *oil on canvas   18⅛ × 21⅝ in.*
*Paris, Musée du Petit-Palais*

# Drawings

SCHOOL OF PARIS  Portrait of Louis II of Anjou, about 1410-15
*pen and watercolor*  *12 × 8½ in.*
*Paris, Bibliothèque Nationale*

JEAN FOUQUET   Portrait of Juvenal des Ursins, about 1450   *black chalk*   *10½ × 7½ in.*
*West Berlin, Kupferstichkabinett*

MASTER OF MOULINS  Portrait of a Woman, about 1490  *pen*  $7\frac{1}{4} \times 5\frac{1}{4}$ *in.*
*Paris, Louvre*

**JEAN CLOUET**  Portrait of Odet, Seigneur of Lautrec, 1526  *black chalk   13 × 9 in.*
*Chantilly, Musée Condé*

164

ÉTIENNE DELAUNE  Music  *pen and wash*  $7\frac{7}{8} \times 10\frac{3}{8}$ *in.*
*Paris, Louvre*

FRANÇOIS CLOUET   Charles IX of France, 1561   *black and red chalk*   *13¼ × 8⅞ in.*
*Leningrad, Hermitage*

ANTOINE CARON   Water Fête at Bayonne, 1565   *black chalk and brown ink*   13¾ / 19¼ *in.*
*New York, Pierpont Morgan Library*

TOUSSAINT DUBREUIL   Ceres Looking for her Daughter, about 1600
*pen and wash*   9 × 13⅝ *in.*
*Paris, Louvre*

PIERRE DUMONSTIER II  Portrait of Henri de Lavardin-Beaumanoir (?), 1618
*black and red chalk  13¼ × 10 in.*
*Paris, Bibliothèque Nationale*

JACQUES BELLANGE   The Hunt of the Duke of Lorraine, about 1606   *black chalk, pen and wash   15⅝ × 19⅝ in.*
*Nancy, Musée des Beaux-Arts*

SIMON VOUET  A Seated Woman  *black chalk*  7¼ × 5½ *in.*
*Paris, Louvre*

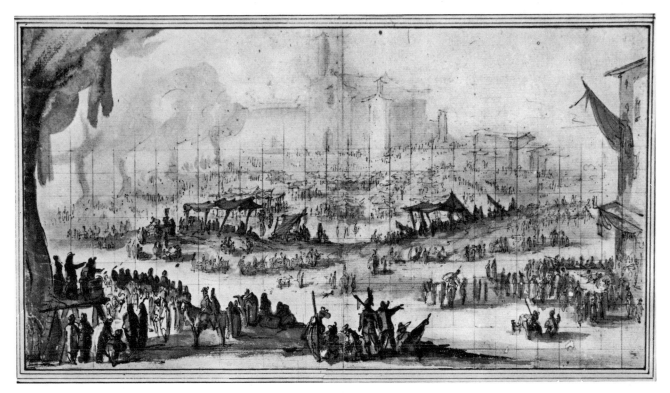

JACQUES CALLOT   The Fair of the Impruneta at Florence, 1620   *black chalk, pen and wash   8 × 15½ in.*
*Vienna, Albertina*

CLAUDE MELLAN  Portrait of Henrietta of England  *black chalk*  $7\frac{1}{4} \times 5\frac{1}{4}$ *in.*
*Stockholm, Nationalmuseum*

NICOLAS POUSSIN   The Massacre of the Innocents   *pen and wash*   $5\frac{3}{4} \times 6\frac{3}{4}$ *in.*
*Lille, Palais des Beaux-Arts*

NICOLAS POUSSIN   The Bearing of the Cross, about 1645   *black chalk and wash*   $6\frac{1}{2} \times 9\frac{7}{8}$ *in.*
*Dijon, Palais des États de Bourgogne*

CLAUDE GELLÉE LORRAINE   The Tiber above Rome   *wash*   $7 \times 10\frac{5}{8}$ *in.*
*London, British Museum*

GASPARD DUGHET or GASPARD POUSSIN  A Wood and Stream  *pen and wash*  *10½ × 16 in.*
*London, British Museum*

EUSTACHE LE SUEUR  The Muse Erato  *black chalk*  *15 × 9¼ in.*
*Paris, École Nationale des Beaux-Arts*

CHARLES LEBRUN  The Apotheosis of Hercules, about 1650  *black and red chalk*  *12¾ × 18⅛ in.*
*Paris, Louvre*

ROBERT NANTEUIL   Portrait of Gilles Menage, 1652   *chalk*   6½ × 4¾ *in.*
*London, British Museum*

ANTOINE WATTEAU   A Seated Woman, about 1716   *red chalk*   $7\frac{7}{8} \times 7\frac{3}{4}$ *in.*
*Chantilly, Musée Condé*

ANTOINE WATTEAU   Four Studies for Italian Comedians
*red and black chalk with white crayon   10¼ × 15½ in.*
*Chicago, Art Institute*

FRANÇOIS BOUCHER   Sea God and Water Nymphs   *red and white chalk   11½ × 18⅜ in.*
*Paris, Louvre*

GABRIEL JACQUES DE ST. AUBIN  A Group of People in a Park  *pen and wash heightened with white*  $12\frac{3}{8} \times 10\frac{1}{4}$ *in.*
*Leningrad, Hermitage*

JEAN BAPTISTE GREUZE   A Seated Nude
*red chalk*   $17\frac{1}{2} \times 14\frac{1}{2}$ *in.*
*Cambridge, Mass., Fogg Art Museum*

JEAN HONORÉ FRAGONARD
The Pasha
*pen and wash*   $9\frac{5}{8} \times 14\frac{5}{8}$ *in.*
*Paris, Louvre*

JEAN HONORÉ FRAGONARD   The Big Cypresses of the Villa d'Este, about 1760
*red chalk*   *18⅞ × 13⅞ in.*
*Besançon, Musée des Beaux-Arts*

HUBERT ROBERT   Madame Geoffrin in her Boudoir   *black chalk*   $11\frac{1}{4} \times 9\frac{1}{4}$ *in.*
*Valence, Musée des Beaux-Arts*

PIERRE PAUL PRUD'HON  A Nude with an Uplifted Arm  *black chalk heightened with white*  $11 \times 8\frac{1}{4}$ in.
*Philadelphia, Pa., collection Henry P. McIlhenny*

JEAN AUGUSTE DOMINIQUE INGRES   The Guillon-Lethière Family, 1815
*pencil and black chalk   10¾ × 8¼ in.*
*Boston, Mass., Museum of Fine Arts*

JEAN AUGUSTE DOMINIQUE INGRES
Study for The Golden Age at the Château
de Dampierre  *pencil  11¼ × 5¼ in.*
*London, British Museum*

THEODORE GERICAULT  A Negro Soldier  *pencil and wash*  $13\frac{1}{4} \times 10\frac{1}{2}$ in.
*Cambridge, Mass., Fogg Art Museum*

EUGÈNE DELACROIX   Study for *The Death of Sardanapalus*, about 1827
*red chalk and wash*   $15\frac{3}{4} \times 10\frac{5}{8}$ *in.*
*Paris, Louvre*

JEAN BAPTISTE CAMILLE COROT  A Stream at Civitacastellana, about 1826
*pencil and wash*   *12¼ × 15⅜ in.*
*Paris, Louvre*

PAUL HUET  A Mountain Landscape, 1833   *watercolor*   *8½ × 11¼ in.*
*Montpellier, Musée Fabre*

HONORÉ DAUMIER  A Clown, about 1868
*black chalk and watercolor  14⅜ × 10 in.*
*New York, Metropolitan Museum of Art*

JEAN FRANÇOIS MILLET  The Harvesters' Rest, 1849
*black chalk, watercolor, and pastel  18⅞ × 37¾ in.*
*Paris, Louvre*

THÉODORE CHASSÉRIAU   Portrait of Princess Belgiojoso, 1847   *pencil   12¼ × 9 in.*
*Paris, Musée du Petit-Palais*

# Sculpture

BURGUNDIAN SCHOOL   The Tomb of Philippe Pot, about 1480   *stone   61 × 104 in.*
*Paris, Louvre*

FRENCH SCHOOL   The Magdalen, from the Sepulchre, late 15th century   *stone*
*Solesmes, France, Church*

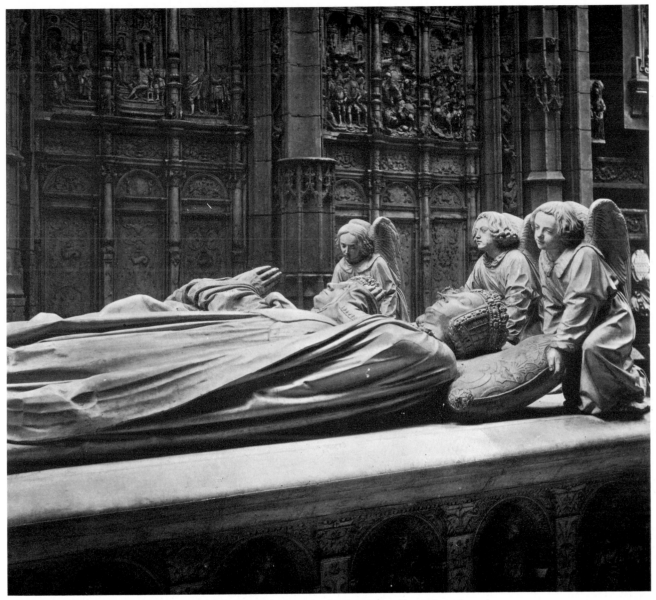

MICHEL COLOMBE   The Tomb of Francis II of Brittany, completed 1507   *marble*   153⅛ × 91¾ × 50 *in.*
*Nantes, Cathedral*

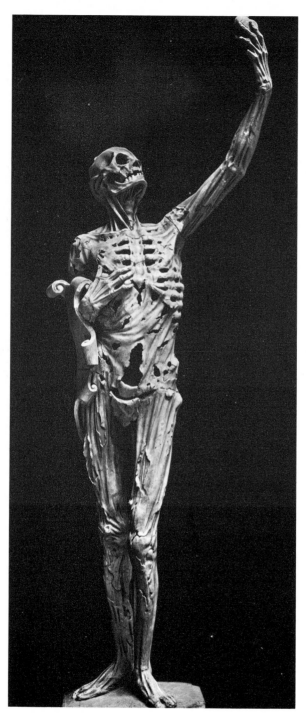

TROYES SCHOOL   St. Martha, about 1510
*marble   height 61 in.*
*Troyes, Church of La Madeleine*

Attributed to LIGIER RICHIER
The Tomb of René de Châlons, after 1544   *stone   height 69 in.*
*Bar-le-Duc, St. Pierre*

JEAN GOUJON  The Fountain of the Innocents, 1547-49  *stone*
*Paris, Place des Innocents*

GERMAIN PILON   The Tomb of Henry II and Catherine de' Medici (detail) 1563-70   *marble   length 69 in.*
*Paris, St. Denis*

JACQUES SARRAZIN   The Tomb of Henry of Bourbon, 1648-63   *marble and bronze*
*Chantilly, Musée Condé*

JEAN WARIN Cardinal Richelieu, about 1640
*bronze height 27½ in.*
*Paris, Bibliothèque Mazarine*

PIERRE PUGET   Milo of Crotona, 1671-83
*marble   height 106 in.*
*Paris, Louvre*

FRANÇOIS GIRARDON  The Rape of Persephone, about 1679  *marble  height 106 in.*
*Versailles, Château Park*

ANTOINE COYSEVOX  The Duchess of Burgundy as Diana. 1710
*marble  height 77 in.*
*Paris, Louvre*

EDMÉ BOUCHARDON  Summer, from the Fountain of the Seasons, 1739-45  *stone*
*Paris, rue de Grenelle, Faubourg Saint-Germain*

**JEAN BAPTISTE LEMOYNE** Noël Nicolas Coypel, 1730 *terracotta* *height 25⅝ in.*
*Paris, Louvre*

MICHEL ANGE SLODTZ  The Tomb of Languet de Gergy, 1753  *marble and bronze*
*Paris, St. Sulpice*

JEAN BAPTISTE PIGALLE  The People, from the Monument to Louis XV, 1758  *bronze and marble*
*Reims, Place Royale*

ÉTIENNE FALCONET  Peter the Great, 1780  *bronze  height 199 in.*
*Leningrad, Hermitage*

CLODION   Bacchante Seated Playing with a Child
*terracotta   height 11⅝ in.*
*Paris, Louvre*

JEAN ANTOINE HOUDON   Sabine Houdon,
about 1790   *plaster   height 20⅞ in.*
*Paris, Louvre*

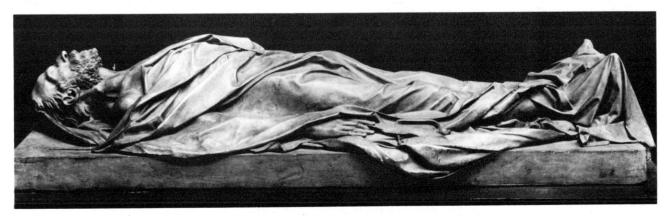

FRANÇOIS RUDE   The Tomb of Cavaignac, 1847   *bronze   15⅜ × 74½ × 25½ in.*
*Paris, Montmartre Cemetery*

ANTOINE LOUIS BARYE  A Jaguar Devouring a Hare, 1850  *bronze*  *17 × 39 in.*
*Paris, Louvre*

JEAN BAPTISTE CARPEAUX  The Fountain in the Luxembourg Gardens, about 1874
*bronze*  *height 82 in.*
*Paris*

# Influences and Developments

*Italian Painters at Avignon in the 14th Century*

During the 14th century the Papal Court at Avignon under Pope Clement VI (1342-52) and Pope Innocent VI (1352-62) reached an unprecedented magnificence and established a vogue for princely patronage that anticipated the 16th century. As a result of its policy artists were drawn from all over Europe. From Italy came the Sienese painter Simone Martini who arrived in Avignon in 1340 and remained there until his death in 1344. He was followed by Matteo Giovannetti who executed the frescoes in the Palace of the Popes.

The originality of the new artistic culture stemmed from the combination of French taste and the impact of the Sienese style and resulted in a courtly decorative style with typical themes: hunting (a), and scenes of courtly love, drawn from the "Roman de la Rose," Petrarch, and other works. The individual portraits in the frescoes of Giovannetti (c) anticipate the independent development of French portraiture (d); a bold pursuit of perspective is also evident.

The Avignon School was of major importance for the spread throughout Europe of the new ideas then developing in Italy, and laid the foundations of the International Gothic style with its emphasis on linear and rhythmic movement in composition.

a

**a** School of Avignon
Hunting with a Falcon, 1343
*fresco*
*Avignon, Palais des Papes*

**b** Simone Martini
The Road to Calvary: from the
Polyptych of the Passion (detail)
about 1341
*tempera on panel  9⅞ × 7¼ in.*
*Paris, Louvre*

**c** Matteo Giovannetti da Viterbo
Scene from fresco decoration
(detail) about 1345
*Avignon, Palais des Papes,*
*Chapel of St. Martial*

**d** Paris School
Portrait of John the Good,
about 1364
*tempera on panel  24 × 16½ in.*
*Paris, Louvre*

b

c

d

## 14th-Century and Early 15th-Century

The end of the 14th century is marked in France by the birth of easel painting. Mural and miniature painting together with the applied arts of stained glass and tapestry, however, remained a privileged and essential part of the artistic achievement of the period.

For example, the great tapestries woven in Paris by Nicolas Bataille for Louis of Anjou, from 1373 onwards, depicting Apocalyptic scenes (a), constitute a pictorial ensemble comparable in monumentality to the most famous Italian fresco cycles.

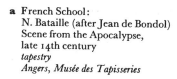

**a** French School:
N. Bataille (after Jean de Bondol)
Scene from the Apocalypse,
late 14th century
*tapestry*
*Angers, Musée des Tapisseries*

**b**

**c**

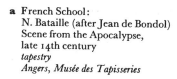



**a**

## The Birth of International Gothic

Between 1380 and about 1425 throughout the whole of Europe common themes and comparable styles may be traced; all are linked to that cultural and artistic trend known as "International Gothic." Paris was one of the foremost centers of this style and its school of painting was certainly the main source for the spread of new ideas and techniques. In Paris the old Gothic tradition of the illuminators was fused with the new and increasing interest in the realism previously introduced by Flemish artists living there.

Franco-Flemish art, as it is portrayed in the Parement de Narbonne (b), assumes the tortured effect of late Northern art combined with a decorative quality which may be indicative of Sienese influence. The sinuosity of the figure style and the linear arrangement in *The Entombment* from the Parement is much modified and softened in (c), the work of a Flemish painter, Jean Malouel, at the court of Dijon, where both Italian and Flemish influences were felt. The gentle treatment of the dead Christ in (b) may be compared to a harsher more brutal statement of the event in a work by the German painter, Master Francke (d). The French picture is characterized by its poise and simplicity whereas the arrangement of the figures in the German work and the figure of Christ in particular are more tense and more charged emotionally. A difference of facial types is also evident.

Links between the art of Paris and the Lombard school were very strong, French and Italian influences having converged at the court of the dukes of Burgundy in Dijon. Daily life at the courts of the aristocracy as opposed to earlier religious themes is depicted in miniature painting, and a similar interest in gracious living, in elaborate and fashionable dress, and in the quiet arrangements of a life of leisure is found at the beginning of the 15th century in both North Italian and French manuscripts. This taste for luxury and refinement in and around both Paris and Milan is illustrated in the miniatures shown in (e) and (f), where the artists portray a non-religious scene of intimate daily life in the familiar courtly surroundings.

In the treatment of a similar theme, however, the *Hortus Conclusus* or enclosed garden (g), (h), and (i), the French artist demonstrates a far greater interest in an elegant, courtly, and predominantly pattern-making or linear conception of his subject, whereas in the work of the German and Italian artists the religious aspect of the theme is more closely adhered to. The elaboration of the background of the French tapestry (g) provides a contrast to the simplified approach of the German and Italian works in (h) and (i).

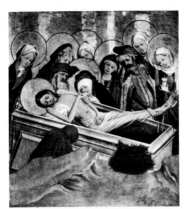

d

e

f

g

h

i

b Paris School
The Entombment:
Scene from the Parement de
Narbonne, about 1373-78
*monochrome on silk*
*Paris, Louvre*

c Attributed to Jean Malouel
Pietà, about 1400
*tempera on panel   diameter 25¼ in.*
*Paris, Louvre*

d Master Francke
The Entombment, about 1425
*tempera on panel   39 × 35 in.*
*Hamburg, Kunsthalle*

e Lombard School
Scene from the Manuscript of
Guiron le Courtois, about 1380
*vellum*
*Paris, Bibliothèque Nationale*

f Paris School
Scene from Hécyse, from the
manuscript of Térence des Ducs
*vellum*
*Paris, Bibliothèque de l'Arsenal*

g French School
The Offering of the Heart,
about 1410
*tapestry*
*Paris, Louvre*

h Master of the Upper Rhine
The Paradise Garden, about 1410
*oil on panel   10¾ × 13¼ in.*
*Frankfurt, Städelsches Kunstinstitut*

i Stefano da Verona
The Madonna of the Rose Garden,
early 15th century
*tempera on panel   50⅜ × 37⅞ in.*
*Verona, Museo di Castelvecchio*

## France and International Gothic

Further comparisons may be made which underline the "international" character of the period and the European exchanges which took place. The French profile portrait of a lady (a) finds a close parallel in that by Pisanello (b). Both French and Italian painters manifest the same taste for luxury, elegance, and fashion and in both works the style is of a decorative, unrealistic character, relying on a graphic delineation of form rather than on a precise rendering of space and volume.

The Wilton Diptych (c), possibly painted for the marriage of Richard II of

a

b

c

**a** French School
Portrait of a Lady in Profile,
about 1420
*tempera on panel  20⅜ × 14⅜ in.
Washington, D. C., National Gallery
of Art, Mellon Collection*

**b** Pisanello
Princess of the Este
Family, about 1438
*oil on panel  16⅞ × 11¼ in.
Paris, Louvre*

**c** The Wilton Diptych, about 1380-90
*tempera on panel  14½ × 21 in.
London, National Gallery*

**d** Master of the Hours of Boucicaut
St. George and the Dragon,
about 1415
*vellum
Paris, Musée Jacquemart-André*

**e** Bernardo Martorell
St. George and the Dragon,
about 1435
*tempera on panel  56 × 38 in.
Chicago, Art Institute, Gift of
Mrs. Richard E. Danielson and
Mrs. Chauncey McCormick*

d

e

England and Isabel of France, may be regarded as a most significant emanation of Parisian style outside France.

A comparison between (d) and (e) reveals how the Catalan imitator of the French work does not invest his subject with the same graceful linear convolutions which typify the greater mannerism of the French approach.

In both (f) and (g) the complicated angular drawing of the figure of the Madonna leads to a certain expressionism. The Master of Heiligenkruz, an Austrian artist, who was perhaps trained in Paris, derives the greatest possible effect from an energetic looping of the drapery folds.

In the same expressionistic style a marked taste for the depiction of death, of suffering, and of the grotesque is found. The violence and intensity of the anatomical drawing and the preoccupation with Death in (h) and (i), derives from the same religious fervour that inspired (f) and (g).

f

g

h

i

**f** Master of the Hours of Rohan
The Madonna and Child,
about 1418-25
*vellum* $11\frac{1}{4} \times 8\frac{1}{4}$ *in.*
*Paris, Bibliothèque Nationale*

**g** Master of Heiligenkruz
The Madonna and Child,
about 1410
*Vienna, Kunsthistorisches Museum*

**h** Master of the Hours of Rohan
The Dead Man before his Judge,
about 1418-25
*vellum* $11\frac{1}{4} \times 8\frac{1}{4}$ *in.*
*Paris, Bibliothèque Nationale*

**i** French School
The Dance of Death, about 1450
*fresco*
*Le Chaise-Dieu, Ėglise Abbatiale*

215

## French Painting in the 15th Century: European Exchanges

The "courtly" International Gothic style ended after 1425. General tendencies in Europe were toward a greater realism and a greater objectivity. Leading this new pictorial analysis of light and form were Jan van Eyck in Flanders and Masaccio in Italy. The purely linear interests and research of International Gothic were now to become a growing preoccupation in the rendering of form and volume. This trend is illustrated by the influence of Burgundian sculpture, particularly that of Claus Sluter (a), on the conception of human form and on the painting of drapery folds found in the work of Conrad Witz (b), and the Provençal painters (c).

a    b    c

d

e

216

Further extensions of this research were the logical grouping of figures in space together with a new awareness of the effects of perspective, as may be seen in (f) and (g). A broader and more exact description of nature was sought after, as in the precision of (e) and (i) and in the analysis of light effects in (h) and (j).

The French art of this period, characterized by the elaborate and balanced style of Jean Fouquet and Enguerrand Quarton, incorporates the influence of Flemish realism and Italian stylization. Its originality derives from this perfect balance between two contradictory tendencies: the Flemish sense of meticulous realism and the Italian sense of plastic synthesis.

Outside these trends French taste remains linked to the ornamental tradition of decorative Gothic elegance as in (d).

**h** Piero della Francesca
The Dream of Constantine (detail)
about 1457
*fresco*
*Arezzo, S. Francesco*

**i** Antonello da Messina
Seascape: detail from
The Crucifixion, before 1465
*oil on panel  23¼ × 9 in.*
*Sibiu, Rumania, Brukenthal Museum*

**j** Master of King René
The God of Love Steals the Heart
of Cuer: from the book of
Coeur d'Amour Épris, about 1460
*vellum  4⅞ × 6¾ in.*
*Vienna, Nationalbibliothek*

f

g

h

i

j

## Painting and Miniatures in the Early 16th Century

At the end of the 15th century and during the beginning of the 16th century there came a period of relaxation in the style of both painters and sculptors. A calm, more restrained form of art developed which harmoniously combined a traditional Gothic style with the later innovations of the Renaissance together with the technical lessons learnt from Flemish painting.

Three major artistic personalities dominate development during this period. The first of these is the Master of Moulins (b), who came under the influence of the Flemish painter, Hugo van der Goes (a), though his rendering of the Annunciation scenes still retains a strong Gothic decorative quality as opposed to the more sculptural conception of the figures used by the Flemish artist.

The two other figures of importance were the illuminators Jean Bourdichon (d) and Jean Colombe (e), in both of whose work may be found an echo of the naïve solidity of Fouquet.

The humanist spirit of the Renaissance penetrated more and more into France after the wars with Italy, as may be seen in the fresco of the Liberal Arts (c), where use of an allegorical subject to decorate a church interior is evidence of this new trend in taste.

**a** Hugo van der Goes
The Annunciation: reverse side
of wing panels of the Portinari
Altarpiece, about 1476
*oil on panel  99⅝ × 118¼ in.*
*Florence, Uffizi*

**b** Master of Moulins
The Annunciation: reverse side
of the wing panels of the Triptych,
about 1500
*oil on panel  61⅞ × 111⅜ in.*
*Moulins, Cathedral*

**c** French School
The Liberal Arts: (from left to right)
Logic, Grammar, Rhetoric, and
Music (detail) about 1500
*fresco*
*Le Puy, Cathedral*

a

b

c

218

The birth of portraiture also takes place in the 16th century in the work of Jean Perréal (f), of Jean Clouet (g), and of Corneille de Lyon (h), where a type of presentation was evolved which lasted until the end of the 16th century. A similar clearcut linear technique and a parallel treatment of the three-quarter view appears in all three works.

d

e

f

g

h

## Fontainebleau and Italian Mannerism

Francis I, himself a great amateur of the arts, wished to make the Court of France a brilliant artistic center; he brought Leonardo da Vinci and Andrea del Sarto to France and purchased works by Raphael. The arrival of Giovanni Battista Rosso (a) in France in 1530 marks the beginning of the School of Fontainebleau. He was followed by two painters from Emilia, Francesco Primaticcio (b), and Niccolò dell'Abbate (c). All three represent the quintessence of Italian Mannerism: Rosso's style is one of strength, even violence and imagination, Primaticcio's is characterized by grace and sensuality, and Niccolò's by a romantic fantasy.

These painters were to find in the rich setting of the French court an atmosphere very favorable to their own work. A life of luxury and moral laxity accompanied by a belief in the teaching of humanism were the order of the day.

a

b

c

d

As a result of their combination with the more realistic styles of certain Flemish or French artists, these Italian tendencies gave birth to an actual School of Fontainebleau, to which works such as (d), (e), and (f) belong. This highly original style in turn exerted a further influence throughout Europe, as may be seen in (g), extending late into the century with the development of the Second School of Fontainebleau as in (h).

e

f

g

h

## The Influence of Caravaggio and Realism in the 17th Century

Following the unreal and fantastic elements which characterized Mannerist painting, a general need for realism in art developed throughout Europe. Caravaggio, the champion of naturalism, influenced the numerous French painters who went to receive instruction in Rome between the years 1620 and 1630. These include such artists as Le Valentin, Simon Vouet, Claude Vignon, and Nicolas Tournier.

In (c), (d), and (g) is found a typical theme of the Caravaggesque School, *The Denial of Saint Peter*, painted by Bartolommeo Manfredi, a pupil of Caravaggio, in (c) and by two French painters, Le Valentin (d), and Georges de La Tour (g). In

a

b

c

d

all three works the religious scene is treated with the same realism, naturalism, and sense of immediacy. The presentation of the figures is based on a broad, close-up arrangement within a limited space in order to emphasize their reality. The nocturnal setting and lighting of the scene also accentuate these qualities.

The evolution of the Caravaggesque movement throughout the century was characterized above all by its Romanticism and a taste for violence among the younger painters in Rome (a). Once assimilated in France it became sober, austere, and classical, especially in a provincial setting such as Toulouse (b). Alternatively it developed into an intense yet restrained naturalism (e) and in provincial art paved the way toward a violent, modern vision of reality (f) and (h).

f

e

g

h

## Grand Decoration in the 17th Century

In illustrations (b), (d), and (g), are found the three principal types of grand ceiling decoration in France in the 17th century. In (b) and (g) may be seen the development of church ceiling painting during the century and in (d) is demonstrated the type of grandiose decoration found in state apartments of the period. The first (b) was influenced by a similar type of gallery found in Italy in the 16th century; the second (d) is derived from the painting of earlier galleries in Rome. These provided models for the painted galleries executed throughout Europe

**a** Simon Vouet
The Presentation in the Temple,
1641
*oil on canvas* 154¾×98¾ *in.*
*Paris, Louvre*

**b** Martin Fréminet
The Fall of Angels: from the ceiling
of the Chapel of the Trinity,
begun 1608
*fresco*
*Fontainebleau, Château*

**c** Simon Vouet
The Rape of Persephone,
about 1640
*tapestry*
*Paris, Hôtel Sully*

a

b

c

during the 18th century. The third example (g), the ceiling of the chapel of Versailles, illustrates the influence in France of the grand illusionistic decor of Roman Baroque in which the architectural elements of the ensemble are incorporated in the design to a greater degree than is found in earlier decoration.

The decorative role played by tapestries in the embellishment of the great reception rooms of the 17th century are illustrated in (c) and (f). In (f) an elaborate use is made of illusionistic architectural and landscape devices equivalent to the same techniques found in painting.

The large altar pictures illustrated in (a) and (e) are manifestations of a modified Baroque style. The combination of rich architectural design and the grandeur of religious decoration which together represent the Baroque are both to be found in (d).

d

e

**d** Charles Lebrun
Mercury: detail from the
Hall of Mirrors, 1671-81
*fresco*
*Versailles, Château*

**e** Jean Jouvenet
The Death of St. Francis,
about 1714
*oil on canvas   81¼ × 59 in.*
*Rouen, Musée des Beaux-Arts*

**f** Charles Lebrun
The Month of June,
late 17th century
*tapestry*
*Fontainebleau, Château*

**g** Antoine Coypel
The Ceiling of the Chapel, 1708
*fresco*
*Versailles, Château*

f

g

225

## *From the Bolognese to Flemish influence in the 17th Century*

During the course of the 17th century, French painting remained open to foreign influences. These derived from three sources: firstly, from French painters resident in Italy or traveling there while studying such as Le Valentin, Claude, and Nicolas Poussin; secondly, from Italians working in France, as for example Orazio Gentileschi, Giovanni Francesco Romanelli, and Gian Lorenzo Bernini; and lastly from Flemish painters in France such as Philippe de Champaigne and van der Meulen.

The influence of Bolognese landscape painting (a) may be traced in the compositional structure of the classical French landscape as typified by the work of Nicolas Poussin (b) and Gaspard Dughet. The illusionism of Roman Baroque (d) and certain elements of French Baroque are evident in Pierre Mignard's decoration for the dome of the church of Val-de-Grâce in Paris (e).

a

b

c

d

e

Later in the century the dominant note became that of color and of a Rubensian approach which triumphs over the earlier and more academic approach of Poussin with its emphasis on drawing.

After 1680 the influence of Venetian color (g) is found in the work of the young painters (j), who were weary of the academic style. At the same time the influence of Flemish art (h) is found in the field of still-life (i) and in animal painting. In more general terms, Flemish painting advocates a more painterly technique with a greater emphasis on the richness and freedom of the brush stroke.

A comparison between different types of compositional landscape is seen in (c) and (f): (c) represents a typical classical work of the mid-century whereas (f) demonstrates the broader conception of a panoramic landscape in the Flemish manner.

**g** Paolo Veronese
The Finding of Moses
*oil on canvas*
*Madrid, Prado*

**h** Jan Fyt
Still-life with a Peacock, about 1646
*oil on canvas   54 × 53 in.*
*Vienna, Kunsthistorisches Museum*

**i** François Desportes
Still-life with Flowers, Fruit, and Animals, 1717
*oil on canvas   72½ × 91 in.*
*Grenoble, Musée des Beaux-Arts*

**j** Charles de La Fosse
The Finding of Moses
*oil on canvas   49¼ × 43¾ in.*
*Paris, Louvre*

f

g

h

i

j

## The Grand Manner in Painting and Rococo Decoration in the 18th Century

The Grand Style in painting underwent a parallel evolution in the 18th century. Initially, having inherited the Grand Manner of Lebrun, it is typified by a Baroque strength and emphasis on the heroic as in the work of Jean Jouvenet (a). These characteristics continued in the work of Jean Restout (c), Jouvenet's nephew, and then reappeared with renewed vigor in the painting of Gabriel Doyen (d), before being tempered by Neoclassicism. Such examples concern only monumental religious painting. Secular painting, on the other hand, with the exception of

**a** Jean Jouvenet
The Miraculous Draft of Fishes, 1706
*oil on canvas* $154\frac{3}{8} \times 241\frac{1}{4}$ *in.*
*Paris, Louvre*

**b** François Lemoyne
Study for the ceiling of the Salon d'Hercule, Versailles
*oil on canvas*
*Toulouse, Musée des Augustins*

**c** Jean Restout
The Death of St. Scholastica (detail) 1730
*oil on canvas* $135 \times 74\frac{7}{8}$ *in.*
*Tours, Musée des Beaux-Arts*

**d** Gabriel Doyen
The Miracle of the Devoted Plague-Stricken, about 1767
*oil on canvas* $31\frac{1}{2} \times 19\frac{5}{8}$ *in.*
*Paris, Louvre*

a

b

c

d

228

François Lemoyne, who painted a grand scheme of mythological decoration in the Venetian manner for the Palace of Versailles (b), adopted a Rococo style partly derived from the tapestry by Jean Bérain (e). Rococo decoration glories in the complicated decor of *cabinets* and *boudoirs* where the painting adorns complete areas of panelling (f), or simply decorates overdoor panels and wall sections dividing windows and mirrors (g). Even when interior decoration is simplified during the second half of the century, decorative paintings still remain subjected to their setting and have no monumental function (h).

e

f

g

h

e  Jean Bérain
   The Musicians, 18th century
   *tapestry*
   *Aix-en-Provence, Musée des Tapisseries*

f  Christophe Huet
   Detail of decorative scheme,
   about 1741
   *oil on panel*
   *Chantilly, Musée Condé,*
   *Salon de la Grande Singerie*

g  Charles Joseph Natoire
   Salon de Psyche
   *Paris, Hôtel Soubise*

h  Jean Honoré Fragonard
   The Fragonard Room, South-east
   corner, from 1771
   *New York, Frick Collection*

## Convention and Reality in the 18th Century

The illustrations on pages 228 and 229 provide an aesthetic comparison of the various trends of 18th-century art which existed concurrently with the general historical development. Illustrations (a) to (e) on these pages demonstrate the taste for decoration and conventional *genre* particular to the 18th century whereas illustrations (f) to (j) indicate a persistent tendency toward realism during the same period. This contrast is epitomized in the different approach of examples (a) and (g). The pomp and sumptuousness of the state portrait (a) provides a vivid antithesis in taste to the essential simplicity of the still-life painting of Chardin and Jean

a

b

c

d

e

Baptiste Oudry (g). Parallel differences are to be found in the opposition between the theatrical convention of landscape as it is portrayed in paintings of the *fête galante* type (b), and the precise, direct observation of nature in the landscape by Alexandre François Desportes (f). The exactitude and simplicity of this view of the natural world is found later in the work of Louis Gabriel Moreau (j) and announces the vision of the 19th century. A further revolution in taste and manners reacted against the glossy flattery and simpering grace of court portraiture. The coy smiles of the royal children portrayed in (c) belong to a world that is far removed from the discreet tenderness and more factual approach of certain "painters of realism" whose interests lay with the honest depiction of more modest sitters in a far less flamboyant setting (h). The most obvious opposition is to be found between the inconsequential and pleasing artifice of a hieratic effigy of grace and courtly behaviour (e), and the terrible, agonized reality of revolutionary historical painting, (i). The frivolity of (e) and the intensity of (i) together sum up this contrast inherent in 18th-century French taste.

e  Madame Vigée Lebrun
   Marie Antoinette with a Rose,
   about 1783  *oil on canvas 44⅛ × 34⅝ in.*
   *Versailles, Château*

f  Alexandre François Desportes
   Landscape  *oil on paper  11 × 20⅝ in.*
   *Compiègne, Musée National*

g  Jean Baptiste Oudry
   The White Duck, 1753
   *oil on canvas  37½ × 24¼ in.*
   *London, Cholmondeley Collection*

h  Françoise Duparc
   A Woman Darning
   *oil on canvas  30¾ × 25¼ in.*
   *Marseilles, Palais Longchamp,*
   *Musée des Beaux-Arts*

i  Jacques Louis David
   The Death of Marat (detail) 1793
   *oil on canvas  65 × 50⅝ in.*
   *Brussels, Musées Royaux des Beaux-Arts*

j  Louis Gabriel Moreau the Elder
   The Castle of Vincennes seen from
   the Heights of Montreuil
   *oil on canvas  18¼ × 33⅞ in.*
   *Paris, Louvre*

f

g

h

i

j

**a** Claude Lorraine
View of the Forum, Rome,
about 1630
*oil on canvas 23 × 28⅜ in.*
*Paris, Louvre*

**b** Gaspard Dughet
Roman Baths, about 1670
*oil on canvas 14 × 17⅞ in.*
*London, collection Mr. Denys Sutton*

**c** Hubert Robert
Ruins of the Temple of Paestum
*oil on panel diameter 16¼ in.*
*Amiens, Musée de Picardie*

**d** Joseph Vernet
View of the Palatine Bridge in
Ruins, about 1745
*oil on canvas 15¾ × 30¾ in.*
*Paris, Louvre*

**e** Jean Honoré Fragonard
Waterfalls at Tivoli, about 1765
*oil on canvas 28¾ × 23⅝ in.*
*Paris, Louvre*

## *Italy as Seen by French painters from Claude to Corot*

From Claude onwards until the mid-19th century the Italian countryside and townscape, particularly Rome and the Campagna, remained an important source of inspiration for French painters.

The attraction of Italy was due to the considerable interest shown in the ruins of Roman antiquity and the ample facility these localities provided for atmospheric painting and perspective drawing. Such enthusiasms throughout this period are demonstrated in illustrations (a), (b), (c), and (d). From these interests a type of painting developed in which ancient sites enlivened by scenes of contemporary everyday activities provided the painter with a novel source for work in the picturesque vein, and at the same time enabled him to depict the beauty of the site simply for its own sake.

a

b

c

d

e

The appreciation of the natural scenery as it appears in the work of Jean Honoré Fragonard and Jean Joseph Xavier Bidault (e) and (f) is sometimes modified by a desire to give a dramatic and convincing pictorial account of the effects of light. This is seen in (d) where the structural and compositional elements of the picture take second place to the painter's attempt to capture those contrasts of light and shade which the light of his native country did not provide.

The preoccupation with Italian light and architecture gives these Italian landscapes a calm and essentially classical appearance as is seen in (g), (h), and (i).

The developments reach a climax in the 19th century with the precise realism of the Italian pictures of Ingres (h), which may be contrasted with the atmospheric illusionism of (c). The influence of Italy reached its apogee in the tonal painting of Corot (j).

f

g

h

i

j

a Pierre Subleyras
  The Miracle of St. Benedict, 1744
  *oil on canvas 129 × 84⅝ in.*
  *Rome, S. Francesca Romana*

b Joseph Maria Vien
  The Amorini Vendor
  *oil on canvas*
  *Fontainebleau, Château*

c Benjamin West
  The Departure of Regulus from
  Rome, 1769
  *oil on canvas*
  *London, Kensington Palace,*
  *Royal Collection*

d Louis Gauffier
  The Generosity of the Roman
  Women, 1790
  *oil on canvas 31½ × 44 in.*
  *Poitiers, Musée des Beaux-Arts*

## From Neoclassicism to Romanticism

Neoclassical painting first appeared in Rome as a reaction against the excesses of the Baroque style, especially in the work of the painters Pierre Subleyras (a), Pompeo Batoni, and Anton Raffael Mengs, who sought a more sober and balanced style. This reaction against an earlier style became involved with the Antiquarian movement which had grown up in Rome as a result of the rediscovery of Greco-Roman antiquity through the excavations at Pompeii and the researches of Winckelmann and his circle. The direct influence of Pompeiian motifs is to be found in painting. The setting, costumes, and poses of (b) are derived from such an antique prototype. Apart from these obvious borrowings, painters also exalted in the grandeur of moral heroism in subjects derived from ancient Roman history. Such history pictures are illustrated in (c) and (d), where elaborate groupings of figures are set against classical backgrounds. In some cases, however, antiquity is evoked with a degree of exactitude which gives to the pictures a pretentious quasi-archaeological importance, so rich are the scenes with details of the furniture and

a

b

c

d

decoration, (e) and (f). In David's *Paris and Helen* the figures themselves are dwarfed by the encumbrance of decoration and drapery that surrounds them.

In *The Oath of the Horatii* (g), painted in 1784, and probably the most important French Neoclassical picture, David gives a perfect form to his classicizing tendencies and to his personal theories. Unlike the *Paris and Helen* this picture is the essence of simplicity and severity and the background serves only to emphasize the poses and outlines of the figures. The exactitude and precision of drawing in this work, in which color is entirely subordinated to outline, mark it as a high point of the Neoclassical style.

Simultaneously, within the Neoclassical movement itself, which remained active until 1820, certain subjects appeared which, although completely Romantic in conception, were treated with an entirely Neoclassical technique. The elaborately descriptive detail of (h) and (i) is directly opposed to the precepts of David, as well as the abandonment of subject matter from Roman history, which is exchanged for the realm of fantasy and an extreme variety of historical legend. It is, however, the tumultuous and imaginative atmosphere of these two works which forms the link with later painting.

**e** Gavin Hamilton
Venus Introducing Helen to Paris,
1784
*oil on canvas 129 × 110 in.
Rome, R. Cocchi Collection*

**f** Jacques Louis David
Paris and Helen, 1788
*oil on canvas 57⅞ × 70⅞ in.
Paris, Louvre*

**g** Jacques Louis David
The Oath of the Horatii, 1784
*oil on canvas 130 × 160 in.
Paris, Louvre*

**h** Anne Louis Girodet
Ossian Receiving Napoleon's
Generals, 1802
*oil on canvas 75½ × 71⅝ in.
Malmaison, near Paris, Musée*

**i** Jean Auguste Dominique Ingres
The Dream of Ossian, 1813
*oil on canvas 137 × 108¼ in.
Montauban, Musée Ingres*

e

f

g

h

i

## Romantic Themes

Generally speaking the Romantic painters preferred the exceptional to the usual, and the accidental to the permanent. These preferences appear throughout the choice of subject matter during this period and from them springs a taste for violence and for manifestations of physical power. Energy and physical force are very often symbolized by the horse as in illustrations (b) and (c). In Géricault's work (b), the tone is one of superb military heroism in which man plays a significant role. Delacroix, on the other hand, depicts a drama of animal strength (c), in which man can have no part. The movement of clouds as in (h) is another aspect of the same interest in the flux and drama of a human or natural predicament. Furthermore, the taste of the Romantic painters for heroism (a) is bound up with their enthusiasm for the violence of war subjects, (b). Yet another extension of these interests is a preoccupation with the horrors of death. The campaigns of the

**a**

**a** Boissard de Boisdenier
Episode on the Retreat from Russia, 1835
*oil on canvas*
*Rouen, Musée des Beaux-Arts*

**b** Théodore Géricault
Officer of the Imperial Guard, about 1812
*oil on canvas   $115 \times 76\frac{5}{8}$ in.*
*Paris, Louvre*

**c** Eugène Delacroix
Arab Horses Fighting in a Stable (detail) 1860
*oil on canvas   $26\frac{3}{8} \times 32\frac{1}{4}$ in.*
*Paris, Louvre*

**d** Joseph Mallord William Turner
Stormy Sea with Wreck, late period
*oil on canvas   $39\frac{1}{2} \times 55\frac{3}{4}$ in.*
*London, Tate Gallery*

**e** Paul Huet
The Reef at Granville Point, about 1853
*oil on canvas   $26\frac{3}{4} \times 40\frac{1}{2}$ in.*
*Paris, Louvre*

**b**

**c**

**d**

**e**

Napoleonic era (a), with their combination of human grandeur and misery, were sufficient to fire the imagination of the Romantic artist.

Violence in nature itself, as it is seen in (d) and (e), is perhaps the most typical manifestation of this romantic ideal and is best illustrated in the work of the English painter, Joseph Mallord William Turner (d), whose influence on French painters was considerable.

Their desire to depict the extraordinary led Romantic painters to seek out exotic subjects. The scenes of oriental life in the work of Ingres and Delacroix, (f) and (g) respectively, provided a sense of distance in space and established the orientalism which represents another branch of Romantic taste. The calmness and voluptuousness of these scenes also provides a necessary foil to the wilder, more extreme aspects of Romanticism previously mentioned.

Parallel to this sense of distance in space achieved by Delacroix in his treatment of African subjects, is a similar attitude to the temporal sequence of events that was largely responsible for the wide interest in history painting that grew up in the 19th century. In illustrations (i) and (j) an anecdotal vision of history is demonstrated which would have been unacceptable in earlier periods. As in the subject matter, the painters allow themselves greater freedom of technique. This is evident in the sketch shown in (j).

f

g

h

i

j

f Jean Auguste Dominique Ingres
The Odalisque and the Slave, 1840
*oil on canvas 30 × 41½ in.*
*Baltimore, Md.,*
*The Walters Art Gallery*

g Eugène Delacroix
The Women of Algiers, 1849
*oil on canvas 33⅛ × 43¾ in.*
*Montpellier, Musée Fabre*

h Gabriel Alexandre Decamps
The Defeat of the Cimbri, 1833
*oil on canvas 51¼ × 76¾ in.*
*Paris, Louvre*

i Richard Parkes Bonington
Henry IV and the Spanish
Ambassador to France, 1827
*watercolor 6 × 6¼ in.*
*London, Wallace Collection*

j Eugène François Maria Joseph
Deveria
The Birth of Henry IV of France
(sketch) about 1827
*oil on canvas 25¼ × 21¼ in.*
*Montpellier, Musée Fabre*

## Landscape: from Romanticism to the School of Barbizon

The extreme contrasts of light and shadow in the work of Georges Michel (b), sometimes attain a Rembrandtesque *chiaroscuro*, and the close observation of nature indicates a development in landscape painting later taken up by the Barbizon School. English landscape painting also had an important influence on French landscape painting at the beginning of the 19th century. In 1824 two of Constable's pictures, *The Hay-Wain* (c) and *View of the Stour* were awarded a Gold Medal at the Paris Salon. These two works greatly impressed French painters who also knew the work of the English landscape painter, Richard Parkes Bonington (a), who went out to France as a boy and received his training there.

All these pictures portray a new interest in the precise rendering of natural appearances under actual light conditions. Through the work of Turner and Constable, French painters developed an enthusiasm for weather effects such as the depiction of a storm in (b). The frequent appearance of water subjects, whether the calm millpond of Constable (c), or the careful observation of the Picardy seacoast (a), is another phenomenon typical of this period in art. Later in the century Bonington was to play an important part in the birth of Impressionism, the Impressionist painters having found a close affinity with the analysis of light in Bonington's seascape.

Théodore Rousseau belonged originally to a school of landscape painters who had emerged out of Romanticism and who painted broad, often violent views.

a

b

c

d

e

These artists, Rousseau, Jules Dupré, and Louis Gabriel Eugène Isabey, (f), (d), and (e), practiced a brand of subjective expressionism known as an art of "feeling," characterized by an extreme emotional empathy with the subject. Such works with their all-embracing vision of sea and sky do not, however, have the same impact as the later work of Rousseau (h), in which the themes are more simple and the breadth of vision consciously restrained.

Under the influence of the Dutch 17th-century landscape painters, Rousseau then sought a greater objectivity and realism such as is found in the precise detail and lighting effects of Jacob van Ruisdael (i). The careful delineation of the tree form against a light background of bright sky in the Dutch master is echoed in Rousseau's *A Group of Oak Trees, Apremont* (h) with the trees set in silhouette against the light. All superfluous detail and secondary light effects are eliminated from this canvas, whereas in (f) the billowing mountain sky provides contrasting shadow and color effects.

Rousseau settled at Barbizon in 1844 and encouraged friends such as Diaz de la Peña (g) to pursue a greater realism in landscape.

In the forest of Fontainebleau the Barbizon painters devoted their energies to creating an exact description of peasant life in a rural setting. They painted nature precisely as they saw it.

f  Théodore Rousseau
   View of Mont Blanc, about 1834
   *oil on canvas  56¼ × 94¼ in.*
   *Copenhagen, Ny Carlsberg Glyptotek*

g  Narcisse Virgile Diaz de la Peña
   The Forest of Fontainebleau:
   The Heights of John of Paris, 1867
   *oil on canvas  33⅛ × 41¾ in.*
   *Paris, Louvre*

h  Théodore Rousseau
   A Group of Oak Trees,
   Apremont, 1852
   *oil on canvas  25¼ × 39 in.*
   *Paris, Louvre*

i  Jacob van Ruisdael
   The Bush
   *oil on canvas  26 × 31½ in.*
   *Paris, Louvre*

f

g

h

i

a

a Gustave Moreau
The Dance of Salome
*watercolor*
*Paris, Musée Gustave Moreau*

b Jean Baptiste Carpeaux
Berezowski Attacking the
Tsar Alexander II (sketch)
about 1868
*oil on canvas* $51\frac{1}{8} \times 76\frac{3}{4}$ *in.*
*Paris, Louvre*

c Victor Hugo
Le Bourg in Ruins, 1857
*watercolor*
*Paris, Musée Victor Hugo*

d Adolphe Joseph Thomas Monticelli
Don Quixote and Sancho,
about 1865
*oil on canvas* $38 \times 51\frac{1}{8}$ *in.*
*Paris, Louvre*

## Romanticism under the Second Empire

Even when realistic painting was triumphant throughout France several isolated painters followed a romantic dream.

Such a romantic trend is illustrated in the fantasy and visionary painting of the poet Victor Hugo, who in his watercolor landscapes (c), rejected all semblance of a realistic presentation of nature. His elaborate sketches of gothic-like castles set against turbulent landscapes derive solely from his own vivid imagination.

In the picture of Gustave Moreau (a), a taste for elaborate mythological and Biblical subject matter occurs. These themes are linked to the quasi-religious and historical interests of the Pre-Raphaelites, but unlike the Pre-Raphaelites, Moreau's pictures are executed in a virtuoso technique in which the painter exploits a variety of intense color harmonies and contrasts. His compositions sometimes border on the abstract.

This taste for a violent, unrestrained technique also appears in (b), a composition remarkable for its spontaneity of brushstroke. Such freedom is, in this case, particularly in keeping with the subject, the confusion of the crowd being emphasized by the apparent disorder of the execution. Adolphe Joseph Thomas Monticelli's technique (d), is one of sparkling impasto in which the painter achieves an exaltation of color for its own sake.

b

c

d